Beliefs and Practices: Taking a Fresh Look

Beliefs and Practices: Taking a Fresh Look

Revised Edition

Tom Shipka

ISBN-13: 9781985761117
ISBN-10: 1985761114
Library of Congress Control Number: 2016905306
CreateSpace Independent Publishing Platform
North Charleston, South Carolina

Dedication

To Kate,
who has enriched our journey
beyond measure

A Note to the Reader.

Beliefs and Practices: Taking a Fresh Look is a brief invitation to philosophy. It reflects my belief that far too many people around the world are captives of the social conditioning that they are exposed to, especially as they grow up but also, in many cases, later on. They assume that the beliefs and practices that they learn in the mainstream culture or the subculture to which they belong are well-founded and superior to others. The result is that they conform rather than question. They don't exhibit the curiosity, courage, self-reliance, and self-determination that mark a life worth living.

This book attempts to make the case for intelligent skepticism as a way of life. It includes six chapters. Chapter 1 advocates the need to evaluate prevalent beliefs and practices. The other chapters focus on the key problems in religion (Chapter 2), knowledge (Chapter 3), choices (Chapter 4), right and wrong (Chapter 5), and government (Chapter 6). Each chapter includes a narrative and readings. All but two of the nineteen readings are commentaries I aired on WYSU. The year of a commentary is given next to my name just below the title.

In the revised edition, there are fewer readings, minor changes in each chapter, and, following each chapter, updated *Recommendations for Further Study* and deletion of the *Exercises*.

Tom Shipka
Emeritus Professor of Philosophy
Youngstown State University
tashipka@zoominternet.net

Acknowledgements

I am grateful to my philosophy students at Youngstown State University – nearly 13,000 during a 46-year YSU career – who helped me clarify my thinking, improve my teaching, and get paid for what I loved to do. I am also grateful to the faculty and staff of the YSU Department of Philosophy and Religious Studies for their dedication and productivity over the years.

A thank you also goes to Gary Sexton, Director, and David Luscher, Associate Director, of WYSU, the National Public Radio affiliate at Youngstown State University, who facilitated my commentaries on WYSU from 2005 to 2015. These commentaries are compiled in *Commentaries: 162 Essays on WYSU*, 2018, which is available on Amazon.com.

Tom Shipka

Table of Contents

CHAPTER 1

Introduction

Enculturation and Philosophy

Robert Nozick, a philosopher who taught for many years at Harvard University, told a story about a woman sitting next to him on an airplane who asked him "What do you do for a living?" When he answered, "I'm a philosopher" she said "How exciting! What are some of your sayings?" The stranger on Professor Nozick's airplane is not alone in being foggy about what philosophers do. So let's ask, "What exactly do philosophers do?"

The answer to this question begins with the complex and systematic shaping of a human being from the moment that she is born to make her a functioning member of the culture. Social scientists refer to this social conditioning as *enculturation* or *acculturation*. When a baby is born, it is neither religious nor secular. It prefers neither democracy nor dictatorship. It speaks neither Arabic nor French nor English. It prefers no particular mode of dress or hairstyle. It has a penchant neither for ice hockey nor football nor soccer. It holds no stance on when government may incarcerate a citizen, whether there is an afterlife, whether humans should eat other species of animals, whether a dying person may hasten death, whether there should be honor killings, or where government should draw the line between prudent security measures and overzealous infringement of liberties. As the baby becomes a child, the child an adolescent, and the adolescent an adult, conditioning by family, teachers, peers, religion, the media, and many other influences, will change all this. Eventually, individuals embrace the dominant views on all sorts of issues - beliefs - and the routine patterns of behavior - customs or practices - in the mainstream culture or in their subculture (e.g., street gangs, body art enthusiasts, hackers, Amish, Scientologists, social media devotees, etc.).

Few of us realize how much we're shaped by our surroundings during all phases of our lives. The pressures to conform are as strong as they are silent. Science writer Guy P. Harrison calls these pressures *the bandwagon effect*. (1) He writes:

> You probably think you are an individual who thinks independently and doesn't care too much about what everybody else thinks or does. The truth is, however, we all feel the lure and often succumb to social pressures when it comes to how we eat, dress, talk, buy things, entertain ourselves, *and think*. A good skeptic remembers this when doing an inventory of his or her beliefs and conclusions. *Did I really think this through, or am I just following the herd?* Nothing to be ashamed of here. We all want and need the herd to some degree. Just don't allow yourself to be blinded by this powerful and constant pull on your brain. (2)

The acronym PASS can help us remember why enculturation is so successful. PASS stands for popularity, age, socialization, and satisfaction. We adopt the mix of beliefs and practices that we do because most people whom we know or know about embrace them (**p**opularity), they have been handed down for many years, sometimes generations (**a**ge), we were taught them as we grew up or later on (**s**ocialization), and we find them satisfying, consoling, or fulfilling (**s**atisfaction).

Another factor that figures into the adoption of beliefs and practices is evolution. Scientists tell us that some of our beliefs and practices have been hardwired in us because they promote survival and reproduction. For instance, "believing that there is an invisible agent (God) who sees all and knows all and judges all can be a powerful deterrent" to violating the rules of society. (3) Also, forbidding incest – inbreeding by close relatives – reduces the number of offspring with physical defects. (4)

The fact that a belief enjoys widespread support in a culture, even over an extended period, however, does not guarantee that it is true. History is replete with examples of beliefs, once popular, that have been abandoned. Lo and behold, the sun, not the earth, is the center of our universe. And the cosmos is billions, not thousands of years old. And germs, not the evil eye, cause sickness and disease. Similarly, the fact that a practice is widespread does not guarantee that it is sensible or ethical. Bloodletting, human sacrifice, and slavery, for instance, were commonplace through much of history.

These examples can prompt this objection, however: "You're talking about the distant past. The human race has made great progress over the centuries. Surely, there are no equivalents to these foolish beliefs and harmful practices today!" Really? Consider the following:

- Tens of millions of Americans believe that they can drive safely while using cell phones even though tests show that doing so is tantamount to driving drunk.
- The Gallup organization reports that "More than four in ten Americans continue to believe that God created humans in their present form 10,000 years ago" (5) despite the thoroughly documented findings of science that humans are the product of a complex evolutionary process spanning millions of years. Many of these science deniers oppose the teaching of evolution in our schools or insist that "creation science" or "intelligent design" be taught alongside evolution.
- Forty percent of the U.S. population spends $34 billion a year on the products and services of so-called "alternative medicine" even though there's no proof that they are safe and effective. (6) Further, hundreds of thousands of parents in the U.S. refuse to vaccinate their children, putting them and others at needless risk for measles, mumps, rubella, and other infections. At the prodding of celebrities such as Jenny McCarthy, they believe, without a shred of evidence and contrary to medical science, that vaccines cause autism.
- Most Americans routinely pray for those who are sick or who face other challenges despite the fact that a landmark study found that prayer for others - intercessory prayer - produces no benefit for those prayed for.
- More than two-thirds of U.S. adults are overweight or obese because we routinely consume far more calories than we expend. By doing this we dramatically increase our risks of cancer, cardiovascular disease, diabetes, bone and joint problems, sleep apnea, and stroke. (7)
- Tens of millions of Americans believe that homosexuality is immoral because the Bible condemns it but they ignore the Bible's approval of slavery, the beating and killing of disobedient children, the killing of non-virgin brides, and the subordination of women, and its disapproval of divorce and tattoos.

- Finally, the spread of Ebola in some nations in Africa, including Sierra Leone, Liberia, and Guinea, is fueled by family members and friends washing and dressing the body of the deceased and mourners at the funeral touching it. They follow these practices in accord with an ancient religious belief "to make sure the dead don't return to haunt the living." (8) Government officials and medical professionals, who are struggling to stop these practices, say that they are the cause of a high percentage of the thousands of Ebola-caused deaths in these nations. (9)

Thus, we don't have to look far for foolish beliefs and harmful practices in today's world.

So what does all this have to do with philosophy? The definition of philosophy that we will use in this book is: *Philosophy is the evaluation of beliefs to determine whether they are true and the evaluation of practices to determine whether they are sensible and ethical.* Philosophers, both professionals and amateurs, take a fresh look at beliefs and practices to see whether they are supported by strong arguments and facts.

An *argument* is a string of reasons supporting (or opposing) a belief or practice divided into premises and a conclusion. *Facts* are claims for which there is considerable evidence. Philosophizing requires *skepticism* - a willingness to doubt - and an atmosphere of intellectual freedom.

Unfortunately, there are serious obstacles to philosophy. In some parts of the world, there is a *day-to-day struggle to survive* in the face of violence, famine, oppression, or disease. Here reading, discussion, and debate are unaffordable luxuries.

Next, in all countries, rich and poor, philosophy is threatened by *dogma* – a passionately held faith-based belief that is impregnable to reason and evidence. Dogma infiltrates every segment of every society – family, church, government, civic organization, company, sports team, fan club, social club, political group, service organization – you name it. Dogma thrives in closed societies (e.g., North Korea) where young and old are blocked from access to information and from debate and discussion by custom or law. In closed societies, authorities - political or religious or both - prize conformity over self-determination and perceive skepticism toward received beliefs and practices as treason or heresy. But dogma also thrives in ostensibly open societies. In the United States, for instance, there is overwhelming evidence that Barack Obama was born in the United States and that he is a Christian, not a Muslim. There is also overwhelming evidence that the U.S. is not a Christian nation and that the U.S. Government was not complicit in the 9/11 terrorist attack. Yet millions of Americans passionately deny all this. Let us not overlook religious leaders whose predictions about the end of the world fail time and again, yet most of their followers remain steadfast in their loyalty. In economics, disciples of Milton Friedman and Ayn Rand preach that the free market is the panacea to all of society's ills while Keynesians condemn it as a tool of billionaires to destroy the middle class. When dogma rules, groups reward the faithful, punish dissenters, demonize adversaries, rewrite the past, and exhibit a confirmation bias. A confirmation bias is "the tendency to seek confirmatory evidence in support of already existing beliefs and ignore or reinterpret disconfirming evidence." (10)

Another obstacle to philosophy is *diversions*, especially in more prosperous parts of the world. Hundreds of millions of people are preoccupied with television, the internet, social networks, cell phones, and other electronic devices, which they use mainly for entertainment. For instance, "The average American teen sends and receives more than 3,000 text messages a month" (11) and "...American college students spend, on average, three hours texting and an hour and 40 minutes on Facebook every day." (12) Face-to-face discussion and use of traditional sources of information about the world, such as books, newspapers, and magazines, are endangered species. Indeed, many newspapers have folded and many others are barely hanging on. Research shows that the average American watches more than four hours of TV a day. This adds up to two months of TV-watching a year and nearly eleven years of TV-watching over a 65-year life. In an average U.S. house, a TV is on six hours and forty-seven minutes a day. Two-thirds of U.S. houses have three or more TV sets. (13)

Yet another barrier to philosophy is *early departure from schooling*. In many of our cities, a large percentage of young people – a majority in some cases - drop out before completing high school.

As a result, large numbers of us are ill-informed. Consider these facts:

* Only two out of five of us can identify the three branches of government;
* Less than half of us know which nation dropped the atomic bomb;
* Only one-third of us know that the Congress, not the President, declares war;
* Most of us continue to believe that all terrorists are religious extremists, victims of poverty, members of dysfunctional families, impressionable

youth, mentally ill, poorly educated, or low-achievers, despite studies which show that these are myths;

* A generation ago presidential speeches were pitched at the level of twelfth graders. Today they are pitched at the level of seventh graders;

* Even after the 9/11 Commission stated publicly that Iraq's Saddam Hussein had provided no support to Al Qaeda, a poll showed that half the population still insisted that he had;

* Only 25% of us can name more than one of the five freedoms guaranteed by the First Amendment (speech, religion, press, assembly, and petition for redress of grievances) but more than 50% of us can name two members of the Simpson family (Homer, Marge, Bart, Lisa, and Maggie);

* Only 30% of us know that members of the U.S. House of Representatives serve two-year terms and only 25% of us know that U.S. Senators serve six-year terms;

* Despite the fact that most Americans are Christians, only half of us can name even one of the four Gospels;

* A majority of us cannot name the first book of the Bible;

* Only one-third of us know that, according to the Bible, Jesus delivered the Sermon on the Mount;

* Only one-third of us can identify the founder of a religion other than Christianity; and

* A vast majority of us are unfamiliar with the basic teachings of Islam, the second largest religion in the world after Christianity. (14)

Autonomy and Critical Thinking

The upshot is that philosophy is a stranger to far too many of the more than seven billion people on the planet today. Either they struggle merely to survive, or they live in closed societies, or they prefer dogma to skepticism, or they crave entertainment and wait eagerly for the next reality TV show or the next iteration of their electronic toys, or they abort their schooling. As a result, huge numbers of people don't take a fresh look at their beliefs and practices. They don't take control of their lives. They lack self-direction and independence – what philosophers call *autonomy*, from the Greek for self-legislating or self-directing. An autonomous person accepts the challenge to take a fresh look at his or her beliefs and practices; an autonomous person is intellectually alive and self-confident; an autonomous person is ready and willing to tackle problems and challenges, whether personal or societal; an autonomous person chooses the path of self-reliance, repudiates dogma and mindless conformity, and strives to be a critical thinker. (15) A prime objective of this book is to help readers strive for autonomy.

Footnotes:

1. The term "bandwagon" originally referred to "a usually ornate and high wagon for a band of musicians, especially in a circus parade." The meanings of "bandwagon" that apply to the term's application to social pressures toward conformity, as noted in this chapter, are "a party, faction, or cause that attracts adherents or amasses power by its timeliness, showmanship, or momentum" and "a current or fashionable trend." See *Webster's Ninth New Collegiate Dictionary*, Merriam-Webster, 1991, p. 128.

2. Guy P. Harrison, *Think: Why You Should Question Everything*, Prometheus Books, 2013, p. 81. According to Edward O. Wilson, the bandwagon effect is especially apparent in religion where it explains loyalty to one's own group and hostility to others. This hostility results, he argues, in frequent episodes of violence, including religion-fueled terrorism. See his *The Meaning of Human Existence*, Liveright, 2014, Chapter 13, "Religion," pp. 147-158.

3. Michael Shermer, *The Believing Brain*, Time Books, 2001, p. 167.

4. Shermer, *Ibid.*, p. 238.

5. Frank Newport, "In U.S., 42% Believe Creationist View of Human Origins," June 2, 2014, http://www.gallup.com/poll/170822/believe-creationist-view...

6. See "Americans Spent $33.9 Billion Out-of-Pocket on Complementary and Alternative Medicine," National Institutes of Health News, online.

7. See "Overweight and Obesity in the U.S.," Food Research and Action Center, online; also, "Defining Overweight and Obesity" and "Childhood Obesity Facts," Centers for Disease Control and Prevention, online.

8. *Voice of America News* online, December 21, 2014.

9. *Ibid.*

10. Shermer, *Ibid.*, p. 259.

11. *Time*, February 3, 2014, p. 46.

12. Andrew Reiner, *The New York Times*, November 1, 2013.

13. This information was compiled by TV-Free America, 1322 18th St., NW, Washington, D.C. 20036

14. The points enumerated here are taken from Rich Shenkman, *Just How Stupid Are We? Facing the Truth About the American Voter*, Basic Books, 2008; Stephen Prothero, *Religious Illiteracy: What Every American Needs to Know – and Doesn't*, Harper Collins, 2007; and Robert A. Pape, *Dying to Win: The Strategic Logic of Suicide Terrorism*, Random House, 2005.

15. Thinking is like playing tennis, driving a car, or dieting. It can be done well or badly. In modern education jargon, good thinkers are called critical thinkers. Critical thinkers have a mix of attitudes, skills, and habits that set them apart from sloppy thinkers. On this, see the reading "Are You a Critical Thinker?"

Recommendations for Further Study:

1. *The Power of Belief*, ABC News Special, 10/6/98, S981006-01 (VHS), or 6/3/99, S990603-51 (DVD).

2. Mel Watkins, *Dancing with Strangers: A Memoir*, Simon & Schuster, 1998.

3. Rick Shenkman, *Just How Stupid Are We? Facing the Truth About the American Voter*, Basic Books, 2008.

4. Stephen Prothero, *Religious Literacy: What Every American Needs to Know – and Doesn't*, Harper Collings, 2007.

5. Paul A. Offit, M.D., *Do You Believe in Magic? The Sense and Nonsense of Alternative Medicine*, HarperCollins, 2013.

6. Charles P. Pierce, *Idiot America: How Stupidity Became a Virtue in the Land of the Free*, Anchor Books, 2010.

7. Susan Jacoby, *The Age of American Unreason*, Pantheon Books, 2008.

8. Susan Jacoby, *Never Say Die: The Myth and Marketing of the New Old Age*, Pantheon Books, 2011.

9. Harriett Hall, M.D., "Doctor Bashing Arguments and Their Rebuttals," *Skeptical Inquirer*, Volume 38, Issue 6, November/December 2014, pp. 32-37.

10. *Is Prayer Good for Your Health? A Critique of the Scientific Research*, Heritage Lectures, No. 816, December 22, 2003.

11. *Study of the Therapeutic Effects of Intercessory Prayer (STEP) in Cardiac Bypass Patients...*, American Heart Journal, 2006 April, 151 (4), pp. 934-942.

12. Robert A. Pape, *Dying to Win: The Strategic Logic of Suicide Terrorism*, Random House, 2005.

13. Carol Tavris and Elliot Aronson, *Mistakes Were Made (but not by me)*, Harcourt Books, 2007.

14. James Randi, *Flim-Flam*, Prometheus Books, 1982.

15. Paul Kurtz, *Affirmations: Joyful and Creative Exuberance*, Prometheus Books, 2004.

16. Bob Woodward, *Plan of Attack*, 2004, Simon & Schuster, and *State of Denial*, Simon & Schuster, 2006.

17. Check out James Randi's website: www.randi.org.

18. Michael Shermer, *The Believing Brain*, Times Books, 2011.

19. Chris Hedges, *Empire of Illusion*, Nation Books, 2009.

20. Guy P. Harrison, *50 popular beliefs that people think are true*, Prometheus Books, 2012.

21. Guy P. Harrison, *Think: Why You Should Question Everything*, Prometheus Books, 2013.

22. Check out Michael Shermer's blog at www.skepticblog.org.

23. Juan Williams, *Enough: The Phony Leaders, Dead-End Movements, and Culture of Failure That Are Undermining Black America – and What We Can Do About It*, Three Rivers Press, 2006.

24. Jason L. Riley, *Please Stop Helping Us: How Liberals Make It Harder for Blacks to Succeed*, Encounter Books, 2014.

25. Elena Conis, *Vaccine Nation: America's Changing Relationship with Immunization*, University of Chicago Press, 2014.

26. Edward O. Wilson, *The Meaning of Human Existence*, Liveright, 2014.

27. Bruce Bartlett, *The Truth Matters: A Citizen's Guide to Separating Facts from Lies and Stopping Fake News in Its Tracks*, Ten Speed Press, 2017.

28. Kate Bowler, *Everything Happens for a Reason and Other Lies I've Loved*, Random House, 2018.

29. Diana Nyad, *Find a Way: The Inspiring Story of One Woman's Pursuit of a Lifelong Dream*, Vintage Books, 2015.

30. Charles J. Sykes, *How the Right Lost Its Mind*, St. Martin's Press, 2017.

Readings: Introduction

Cell Phones – A Moral Challenge

Tom Shipka (2009)

I submit a simple moral principle for your consideration. A person who poses an avoidable and unnecessary threat of harm to innocent people should take steps promptly to end the threat.

If you embrace this principle but you use a cellphone while driving, you should stop doing so because cell phones distract drivers and significantly increase the likelihood of accidents. This is clear from the extensive laboratory and road research on drivers and cellphones which was reported this summer in a series of articles in *The New York Times*. (1) Here are some of the revelations in the series:

- In 2003, in order to "avoid antagonizing members of Congress," the National Highway Traffic Safety Administration suppressed research that showed that cellphone usage by drivers was becoming a "serious and growing threat on America's roadways."
- Drivers significantly overestimate their ability to multitask.
- Cellphones are now the number one distraction for drivers in the United States.
- Drivers who use cellphones cause far more fatalities than drivers distracted by all other causes combined.
- Drivers who use cellphones are four times as likely to cause a crash as drivers who do not use them.
- Cellphone users who are sober perform in laboratory tests with the same driving efficiency as drivers who are legally drunk.
- Headsets and other hands-free phones do not materially reduce the risks of a crash because the conversation itself takes a driver's attention off the road.
- Cellphone distractions cause at least 2,000 traffic deaths a year and 330,000 accidents a year.
- In the United States at any given moment, 12% of drivers are using cellphones to talk, text, or e-mail.
- Drivers who text while driving often focus on their screens instead of the road for stretches of more than five seconds.
- Finally, truck drivers who text while driving are 23 times more likely to have an accident than when they are not texting.

One of the ironies surrounding the use of cellphones while driving is that a high percentage of the very same people who acknowledge that using cellphones while driving is dangerous admit that they continue to do so anyhow. This includes people who caused accidents in the past because they were distracted by their cellphones. (2)

Despite the proven dangers of cellphone usage by drivers, there is no imminent prospect of legal reform. Cellphones are so popular that many legislators are reluctant to take a stand for safety over convenience. This year one-hundred seventy bills restricting cellphone usage while driving were introduced in the various states but only ten were adopted. One reason for this is that legislators themselves typically use cellphones while driving. Another is that the cellphone industry lobbies effectively against bans. Moreover, where there are legal restrictions, enforcement is usually lax; for instance, taxi drivers in New York City largely ignore the city's ten-year old ban on the use of cellphones by cabbies and usually the police don't interfere. (3)

So, be proactive. Protect yourself, your passengers, and other drivers. Pull over to a safe spot before you use your cellphone. It is the responsible thing to do. If you wait for government to cower you into doing so, you may wait a long, long time. Meanwhile, thousands of people will suffer or die needlessly. And you or a loved one could be one of them!

1. See *The New York Times*, July 19, 2009, July 21, 2009, July 28, 2009, and August 4, 2009.
2. For instance, see the case of Christopher Hill in *The New York Times*, July 19, 2008.
3. See *The New York Times*, August 4, 2009.

Are You a Critical Thinker? A Test

Tom Shipka (2005)

Thinking is like playing tennis, driving a car, giving a talk, dieting, or speaking a foreign language. It can be done well or badly. In modern education jargon, good thinkers are called critical thinkers. Critical thinkers have a mix of attitudes, skills, and habits that set them apart from sloppy thinkers. Are you a critical thinker? Test yourself by answering these questions. Award yourself a score on each item as high as five (5) or as low as one (1).

1. I am a successful problem-solver._____
2. When I face a problem or mystery, I follow Ockham's Razor, i.e., I seek the simplest adequate solution or explanation instead of a needlessly complex one._____
3. Before I make a decision, I first gather as many relevant facts as time permits and I anticipate the likely consequences of each course of action._____
4. I strive for informed beliefs, that is, beliefs based on solid evidence and sound arguments; I do not embrace beliefs simply because they are popular or consoling._____
5. I appreciate the indispensable role of skepticism in an intelligent and responsible life. I refuse to embrace a claim of adopt a practice, however satisfying or intriguing, until I find reasonable grounds for it.
6. I can explain and defend my beliefs and practices capably._____
7. My beliefs are coherent, that is, some of them don't contradict others._____
8. My practices are coherent, that is, some of them don't contradict others._____
9. My beliefs and practices are coherent, that is, some of the former don't contradict some of the latter._____
10. I use language with precision and clarity._____
11. I am a good listener._____
12. I strive to be objective and even-handed in my assessments. I do not exaggerate the benefits or harms of a belief, a practice, an argument, a person, an organization, a lifestyle, a movement, a product, or a service._____

13. I know that my perceptions can be distorted by my beliefs, expectations, biases, and state of mind._____

14. I know that my memory is selective and constructive and seldom provides a literal report of the past._____

15. I am open-minded and flexible. I am willing to hear or read an elaboration or defense of a position that strikes me initially as weird, foolish, far-fetched, or immoral._____

16. I am sensitive to human fallibility, that is, the fact that humans make mistakes. Accordingly, I have the courage to reevaluate a long-cherished belief or practice and to acknowledge that it may be mistaken._____

17. I am sensitive to human fallibility, that is, the fact that humans make mistakes. Accordingly, I welcome constructive criticism._____

18. I am sensitive to human fallibility, that is, the fact that humans make mistakes. Accordingly, I recognize that well-educated and well-trained persons, even experts, can be mistaken._____

19. I successfully detect bias, special pleading, code words, propaganda, and exaggeration in what I hear or read._____

20. I strive to be honest, fair, and objective. I scrupulously avoid lying and exaggerating, and treating speculation, gossip, or rumor as fact, in order to influence or persuade others._____

21. I am aware that many TV programs, films, and publications deviate from the historical record and contradict well-established scientific laws and theories._____

22. I strive to stay intellectually alive. I regularly read books, newspapers, magazines, and other publications.____

23. I strive to stay intellectually alive. I balance my reading, radio listening, and TV viewing so that I expose myself to a variety of views and perspectives._____

24. I strive to stay intellectually alive. I participate regularly in serious, civil conversations about significant issues facing the human community locally, nationally, and globally._____

25. I detect common fallacies in reasoning such as...
    * Stereotyping (assuming that all members of a group share the same strengths or weaknesses of one or a few members of the group that I observe);

* Hasty generalization (jumping to a conclusion based on insufficient evidence);
* *Ad hominem* (disqualifying a claim or argument based solely on its advocate or supporter);
* The slippery slope (assuming that a modest change will necessarily trigger dire consequences);
* The time fallacy, also called *post hoc ergo propter hoc* (assuming that because one event preceded another, the former caused the latter; confusing correlation with causation); and
* The appeal to ignorance, or shifting the burden of proof (assuming the correctness of a claim or belief simply because it has not been disproven)._____

26. I strive to avoid the use of such fallacies in my own reasoning._____

The highest score possible is 130 points. How did you do? If you are especially bold and brave, you might invite another person who knows you well to evaluate you on this same test, compare the two scores, and discuss any discrepancies. (1)

---

1.   From Thomas A. Shipka and Arthur J. Minton, *Philosophy: Paradox and Discovery*, McGraw Hill, Fifth Edition, 2004, pp. 3-5. This version served as the basis of a WYSU commentary on critical thinking which aired in 2005.

Mistakes Were Made (but not by me)

Tom Shipka (2008)

In 2006 Oprah Winfrey endorsed a book by James Frey which was purported to be a memoir of his drug addiction and recovery. It is entitled *A Million Little Pieces*. Oprah's endorsement made the book an instant best-seller. As time passed an investigative website called "The Smoking Gun" and a journalist named Richard Cohen showed that Frey's story was fabricated. Initially Oprah reasserted her support for Frey. (1) The fact is that Oprah had been duped but she was intent on justifying her original decision and her credibility despite the facts. Remarkably, though, she made a 180 degree turnabout, publicly declared that Frey was a liar, apologized to the journalist, and chastised Frey in front of a national TV audience. (2)

Do most of us show the courage and candor which Oprah showed? No, say Carol Tavris and Elliot Aronson, psychologists and co-authors of a book entitled *Mistakes Were Made (but not by me)*. Their book draws from hundreds of research studies of how people deal with their mistakes. It shows that most of us, to maintain our confidence and self-esteem, routinely fail to admit our mistakes and reject information that questions our beliefs, decisions, or preferences. We thrive on self-justification at the expense of truth.

Early in the book, Tavris and Aronson cite a well-known recent example of a failure to admit mistakes. (3) The Bush administration sold the invasion of Iraq to the nation and the Congress on two principal claims, that Saddam Hussein possessed weapons of mass destruction and that he aided and abetted international terrorism. Both proved to be groundless. Not only did the White House fail to acknowledge this, but it shifted to new justifications for the invasion. (4)

Tavris and Aronson show how bias and self-deception infiltrate all of our relationships, personal and professional. One of the most illuminating chapters is on marriage. It should be mandatory reading for all couples planning to start or end a marriage. The authors point out that stable, lasting marriages are only possible when a person is able "to put empathy for the partner ahead of defending their own territory" and able "to listen to the partner's criticisms, concerns, and suggestions undefensively." (5) Tavris and Aronson marshal persuasive evidence that successful marriages have "a ratio of five times as many positive interactions (such as expressions of love, affection and humor) to negative ones (such as expressions of annoyance and complaints)." (6) Once the "magic ratio" dips below 5 to 1, the marriage is in trouble. (7)

As one reads *Mistakes Were Made*, one wonders if people can let go of self-justification and admit mistakes. The authors insist that with an effort we can and they furnish impressive examples of public figures who have done so. They tell us that the first steps to success are being aware of the tendency to self-justify (8) and reminding ourselves regularly that we are fallible, that is, likely to make mistakes. (9) Finally, a warning. If your experience in reading *Mistakes Were Made* matches mine, you'll be surprised, and perhaps embarrassed, to find yourself in the stories that it tells. (10)

1. Oprah said "The underlying message of redemption in James Frey's memoir still resonates with me..." and she blamed any problems on the publisher. See Carol Tavris and Elliot Aronson, *Mistakes Were Made (but not by me)*, Harcourt Books, 2007, p. 214. All references are to this book.

2. Page 215.

3. Pages 18-19.

4. The new justifications included "getting rid of a 'very bad guy,' fighting terrorists, promoting peace in the Middle East, bringing democracy to Iraq, increasing American security, and finishing 'the task (our troops) gave their lives for.'" On the claim that the U.S. is in Iraq to fight terrorists, a report issued by sixteen U.S. intelligence agencies concluded that "the occupation of Iraq had actually *increased* Islamic radicalism and the risk of terrorism." Page 3.

5. Page 180.

6. Page 173.

7. Page 173.

8. They write: "The need to reduce dissonance is a universal mental mechanism, but that doesn't mean we are doomed to be controlled by it. Human beings may not be eager to change, but we have the ability to change, and the fact that many of our self-protective delusions and blind spots are built into the way the brain works is no justification for not trying... An appreciation of how dissonance works, in ourselves and others, gives us some ways to override our wiring. And protect us from those who can't." (Pages 222-223).

9. Page 228.

10. As *The Wall Street Journal* observes, the book is "by turns entertaining, illuminating and - when you recognize yourself in the stories it tells - mortifying." (Book Cover)

CHAPTER 2

Religion

An Overview

Among the belief systems of the world which are called *religions* are Baha'i (12), Buddhism (4), Christianity (9), Confucianism (6), Hinduism (1), Islam (10), Jainism (7), Judaism (3), Shinto (5), Sikhism (11), Taoism (8), and Zoroastrianism (2). The number next to each is the estimated age of each compared to the others. Hinduism is oldest (#1), Zoroastrianism is next oldest (#2), and so on. There are sharp differences among these religions and, what's more, there are sharp differences within them because each has divisions. Further, we can add many other groups, each unique, to this list (Latter Day Saints, Rastafari, Scientology, Druidism, Jehovah's Witnesses, Wicca, Macumba, Hare Krishna, Unification Church, etc.) This diversity explains why it is so difficult to formulate a consensus definition of religion.

Nevertheless, religions have common features. They embrace a set of beliefs and they follow a set of practices, typically with great conviction and passion. Further, they proclaim a moral code. Finally, importantly, they rest heavily on faith. (1) Faith is "firm belief in something for which there is no proof." (2) In this chapter, we will address three questions that touch on faith:

- *Is it responsible for humans - supposedly rational animals - to opt for faith over reason?*
- *Can the central belief of most religious people - that there is a God – be established through rational arguments?*
- *Does the abundance of suffering in the world amount to a disproof of the belief in an all-powerful and all-good God?*

Reason and Faith

In a daily newspaper that I read, some of the obituaries show a photo of a married couple with the caption "together again" after the death of the second partner and others say that a person who died "went home to heaven to be with the Lord." Do people actually survive their deaths to join their mates and God in heaven? Billions say "YES!" And are they sure of this because they can prove it? No. They are sure of it because of PASS – popularity, age, socialization, and satisfaction! (See Chapter 1.) In other words, they take it on faith.

Certainly most of us would be unlikely to take a lot of claims on faith. For instance, if you were told by a car dealer that a 10-year old used car that you were considering buying had only 5,000 original miles, was never in an accident, spent nearly its entire life in Florida, got every scheduled maintenance on time, and had only one owner - "a little old lady who drove only to the store and to church" - you would insist on documentation. And, if a vendor at a flea market tried to sell you a watch that she claimed was owned by President John F. Kennedy at the time of his assassination, you would insist that it be authenticated by an expert before you bought it.

When it comes to religion, however, skepticism usually retreats and faith takes over. Sam Harris, a neuroscientist who is often grouped with Daniel Dennett, Richard Dawkins, and the late Christopher Hitchens as "the new atheists," notes this tendency in the following passage:

> Tell a devout Christian that his wife is cheating on him, or that frozen yogurt can make a man invisible, and he is likely to require as much evidence as anyone else, and to be persuaded only to the extent that you give it. Tell him (however) that the book that he keeps by his bed was written by an invisible deity who will punish him with fire for eternity if he fails to accept its every incredible claim about the universe, and he seems to require no evidence whatsoever. (3)

The fact is that most of us are skeptics in some cases but not others. Are we acting responsibly when we do this? Is it OK to shift between skepticism and faith? Let's retreat to the nineteenth century when two intellectual giants squared off on this very issue.

In 1876, W. K. Clifford (1845-1879), a mathematician, gave a talk to the Metaphysical Society in London entitled *The Ethics of Belief*. He began with a story about a ship owner:

Doubts had been suggested to him that possibly she was not seaworthy. These doubts preyed (sic) upon his mind, and made him unhappy; he thought that perhaps he ought to have her thoroughly overhauled and refitted, even though this should put him to a great expense. Before the ship sailed, however, he succeeded in overcoming these melancholy reflections. He said to himself that she had gone safely through so many voyages and weathered so many storms that it was idle to suppose she would not come home safely from this trip also. He would put his trust in Providence, which could hardly fail to protect all these unhappy families that were leaving their fatherland for better times elsewhere. He would dismiss from his mind all ungenerous suspicions about the honesty of builders and contractors. In such ways he acquired a sincere and comfortable conviction that his vessel was thoroughly safe and seaworthy; he watched her departure with a light heart, and benevolent wishes for the success of the exiles in their strange new home that was to be; and he got his insurance-money when she went down in mid-ocean and told no tales. (4)

Where did the ship owner go wrong? According to Clifford, although he sincerely believed that the ship was safe,

(H)e had no right to believe on such evidence as was before him. He had acquired his belief not by honestly earning it in patient investigation, but by stifling his doubts.

Further, Clifford notes that our beliefs are "not a private matter." They translate into actions which can cause harm to self or others. This harm can be physical, as in Clifford's story, or mental. On the latter, Clifford observes:

Every time we let ourselves believe for unworthy reasons, we weaken our powers of self-control, of doubting, of judicially and fairly weighing evidence.

Further, Clifford argues, since we are social creatures, constantly interacting with others, when we believe on insufficient evidence, when we believe prematurely, we authorize others to do so. We thereby perpetuate low standards, gullibility, and superstition in society. To avoid this, Clifford argues, we must understand that "(I)t is wrong always, everywhere, and for anyone to believe anything upon insufficient evidence" and that we have a "duty of questioning all that we believe." Whether a belief that you hold has virtually universal support, whether the belief has been held "sacred" for centuries, whether you've been taught the belief since you were a child, and whether you find consolation in the belief, are irrelevant considerations, according to Clifford. Intellectual honesty recognizes only one relevant consideration: *Is the belief true?* (5)

When Clifford's talk was published, it was read by American philosopher and psychologist, William James (1842-1910), who took issue with its insistence on the need for evidence before one adopts a belief. He crafted a rebuttal in which he made the case for faith. As with Clifford, James presented it first to an audience – the philosophy clubs of Yale and Brown. Later, it was published. (6) Early in his talk, James told the students and professors that "I myself find it impossible to go with Clifford." Instead, he said:

> I have brought with me to-night (sic) something like a sermon on justi-
> fication by faith to read to you, - I mean an essay in justification *of* faith,
> a defense of our right to adopt a believing attitude in religious matters,
> in spite of the fact that our merely logical intellect may not have been
> coerced. 'The Will to Believe,' accordingly, is the title of my paper.

James concedes that we have a responsibility to seek truth and shun error. On routine issues, we should never support a view in the absence of evidence. Absent evidence, he says, neutrality is the responsible stand in such cases:

> Wherever the option between losing truth and gaining it is not momen-
> tous, we can throw the chance of *gaining truth* away, and at any rate save
> ourselves from any chance of *believing falsehood*, by not making up our
> minds at all till objective evidence has come. In scientific questions, this
> is almost always the case; and even in human affairs in general, the need
> of acting is seldom so urgent that a false belief to act on is better than no
> belief at all... Throughout the breadth of physical nature facts are what
> they are quite independently of us, and seldom is there any such hurry
> about them that the risks of being duped by believing a premature theory
> need be faced. The questions here are always trivial options, the hypothe-
> ses are hardly living (at any rate not living for us as spectators), the choice

between believing truth or falsehood is seldom forced. The attitude of skeptical balance is therefore the absolutely wise one if we would escape mistakes.

Note the terms *momentous, living,* and *forced* in this passage. They are clues to his justification of faith. An option, where two hypotheses are at odds, is a *genuine* option for you if the hypotheses are momentous and not trivial, living and not dead, and forced and not avoidable. If you face a genuine option and you find insufficient evidence to prove the truth of either hypothesis, you may believe the one that you want to believe, allowing your feelings to take over. Here are James's words:

> The thesis I defend is, briefly stated, this: *Our passional nature not only lawfully may, but must, decide an option between propositions, whenever it is a genuine option that cannot by its nature be decided on intellectual grounds...*

James believed that a genuine option for most people that cannot be resolved "on intellectual grounds" is "There is a God" versus "There is no God." He felt that most of us wish to affirm the former and he gave us the green light to do so. After all, "There is a God" hasn't been proven false, we'll be happier believing than not believing, and, as time passes, *"faith in a fact can help create the fact."* As we act on our belief in God, we may have experiences which confirm it.

Clifford died of tuberculosis before he could reply to James. Had he lived, I suspect that he would say something along these lines:

> Mr. James, you tell us that "faith in a fact can help create a fact." I fully agree with you that we often need to adopt a hypothesis as provisionally true and act upon it to see if we're right. Scientists do it all the time. Also, we often need to have confidence in our hypothesis. For instance, if George goes on a diet, he does indeed need to have confidence at the start that he has the willpower to lose weight. As George weighs himself day after day, he knows what counts as evidence *for* and *against* his hypothesis. But this isn't the case with religious beliefs. Believers don't tell us what counts for and what counts against their belief in God. In fact, they are unlikely to acknowledge that any evidence counts against it.

Beyond this, Mr. James, you are basically saying that a person who wants to believe in God may do so because no one has proven that there is no God. But isn't this the argument from ignorance? Aren't you assuming the correctness of a claim because it has not been disproved. Your approach allows me to proclaim the existence of ghosts, fairies, and leprechauns. If I want to believe in them I may because no one has proven that they don't exist.

Next, setting aside the question of how one would go about disproving the existence of something, it clearly seems to me that you are shifting the burden of proof from the believer to the skeptic. The burden of proof rests with the person who advances a claim. He has the responsibility to show that it has merit, that it is based on strong arguments and well-established facts. You haven't done that.

Further, you're confident that no one has yet proven the non-existence of God. But how can there be a divinity whose power and goodness have no bounds in the midst of deformed newborns, tsunamis, pedophiles, and dementia?

Finally, while you trumpet the many blessings of religion to believers, you ignore its dark side. Religion often exacerbates conflict and violence, sanctions moral outrages, and fosters intolerance. If religion is a blessing, it is a mixed one.

God – The Debate

If we put faith aside and take on Clifford's challenge to embrace a belief only if there is sufficient evidence to support it, will we find that the statement "There is a God" meets his standard? That's what we'll investigate here. We'll study and evaluate a variety of traditional arguments for the existence of God.

The Ontological Argument

One of the oldest arguments, called the *ontological* argument from the Greek terms for science of being, was formulated in different ways by Anselm (1033-1109), Archbishop of Canterbury in England, and Rene Descartes (1596-1650), French philosopher and mathematician.

Anselm, already a believer, turned to reason to reinforce and strengthen his faith. His argument, given in the *Proslogion*, holds that when we form an idea of God, which he is confident that we do, we implicitly prove that God exists. We can paraphrase his argument this way:

We believe that God is a perfect being, *a being greater than which none can be thought*. When we hear or see the term God we (a) understand the term and (b) form an idea of God. To have an idea of God, though, implies the actual existence of God apart from the idea of God in our mind. Why? Because if God existed only in our mind, God would not be the greatest being of which we can think for we can easily think of one that is greater, that is, one that exists both in our mind and apart from our mind. (7)

As for Descartes, in his *Meditations*, which we will explore further in Chapter 3: Knowledge, Descartes offered two arguments similar to Anselm's. In the first one, he claims to have an idea of God, the perfect being, and he asks how this idea arose in his mind. He explains:

By the word 'God' I understand some infinite substance, which is independent, supremely intelligent and supremely powerful, and by which both I, and everything else that exists (if anything else exists), were created. All these ideas are surely such that, the more carefully I examine them, the less likely it seems that they could have originated from myself alone. Therefore one should draw the conclusion from what has been said that God necessarily exists. And even though I have an idea of a substance from the very fact that I am a substance myself, it would not, however, be an idea of an infinite substance because I am finite, unless it originated from some substance that is genuinely infinite. (8)

Here Descartes argues that he, a finite (limited) being, cannot possibly have caused the idea of God, an infinite (unlimited) being, to arise in his mind. So, what caused it to do so? Only an actually existent infinite being could do so.

Next, Descartes insists that when he forms an idea of God, he grasps the *essence* (nature) of God as a perfect being. This, he argues, entails the existence of God because "existence is a perfection." He writes:

But it is clear to whoever thinks about it more carefully that existence can no more be separated from God's essence than one can separate, from the essence of a triangle, that the three angles are equal to two right angles, or than one could separate the idea of a valley from the idea of a mountain. (9)

For Descartes, it is logically impossible to think of "a supremely perfect being" as not existing.

Two issues are pertinent to the viability of the ontological argument. The first is whether we can form an idea of God. The second is whether, if we do, our idea implies that there is a God.

On the first point, philosophers who support *Empiricism* (from the Greek word for the senses) argue that all of our ideas originate in sense experience – what we see, hear, smell, taste, and touch. But what about our ideas of mermaids and unicorns? We don't actually perceive them. Empiricists reply that our imaginations can combine and embellish sensory impressions. The implication of Empiricism for ideas of God is two-fold:

1. Believers tell us that God is a non-physical being but our senses can only grasp physical ones. Since it is therefore impossible to for us to sense God, it is impossible for us to form an idea of God. (Descartes' claim in the *Meditations* is that his idea of God did not arise from his senses but is "innate," or inborn, planted in his mind by God.)
2. People who tell us that they have an idea of God actually have an idea drawn from their experience, which they embellish with the aid of imagination, such as a person (perhaps an actor in a film or a man on a cross), or a powerful force in nature, such as a hurricane, tornado, or tsunami, and not a literal idea of the spiritual, eternal being called God.

On the second point, critics say that the argument errs in treating existence as a predicate. What does this mean? In a sentence the predicate is what is said about the subject. If I say that George is *tall*, the subject is George and the predicate is tall. Here I am attributing the feature tall to George. In this sentence "is" is simply the copula, the link between George and tall. The same is true if I say that George is *handsome*. The subject of the sentence is George and the predicate is handsome. Here, again, I am attributing a feature to George. Likewise, in this sentence "is" is simply the copula, the link between George and handsome. However, when I say George *exists* or George *is*, George is the subject, followed by "is," a link, but the link links nothing to George. In this sentence, there is no predicate. I don't attribute any feature to George. Similarly with God, if I say that God is *compassionate*, I am attributing a feature to God, but if I say that God *is*, I am attributing nothing to God. The upshot is that from an idea of "X" we cannot determine that "X" exists.

The ontological argument is grist for logicians, semanticists, and other specialists. I discuss it here largely for historical value. It certainly hasn't sent thousands to or from churches, temples, and synagogues! Let's move on to arguments which have had far more traction in the mainstream. (We'll return to Descartes later, in Chapter 3.)

The Cosmological Argument

Many influential writings or speeches are quite short. One thinks, for instance, of the Sermon on the Mount, the Declaration of Independence, the Gettysburg Address, and Dr. King's "I Have a Dream" speech. In the world of philosophy, one brief passage that is among the most widely read, discussed, and debated in history is Thomas Aquinas' (1225-1274) five proofs for the existence of God, which take up a mere two pages in his famous *Summa Theologica*. Having rejected Anselm's ontological argument, Aquinas proposed that we look for clues to the existence of God in the world we inhabit and observe with the aid of our senses. His five arguments, the *quinta via*, based on the work of the pagan and polytheistic philosopher Aristotle, are called *cosmological* arguments, from the Greek terms meaning the investigation or study of the cosmos, because they aim to demonstrate the existence of God from God's effects in the cosmos – motion, causality, contingency, gradation, and design.

The cosmological argument is often called the argument from *First Cause* because each of the five versions reasons to the need for a first cause, itself uncaused, which we call God. We can see this in Aquinas' second argument, the one from cause and effect:

> The second way is from the nature of efficient cause. In the world of sensible things we find there is an order among efficient causes. There is no case known (neither is it, indeed, possible) in which a thing is found to be the efficient cause of itself; for so it would be prior to itself, which is impossible. Now in efficient causes it is not possible to go on to infinity, because in all efficient causes following in order, the first is the cause of the intermediate cause, and the intermediate cause is the cause of the ultimate cause, whether the intermediate cause be several, or one only.

Now to take away the cause is to take away the effect. Therefore, if there be no first cause among efficient causes, there will be no ultimate, nor any intermediate, cause. But if in efficient causes it is possible to go on to infinity, there will be no first efficient cause, neither will there be an ultimate effect, nor any intermediate efficient causes; all of which is plainly false. Therefore it is necessary to admit a first efficient cause, to which everyone gives the name of God. (10)

What does Aquinas mean by "efficient" cause? His understanding of causes comes from Aristotle who identified four causes: material, formal, efficient, and final. Let's say that you adopt an abandoned dog - Lucky - and that you build Lucky a dog house in your backyard. For Aristotle, the material cause is the raw materials (nails, wood, shingles, etc.) that you use, the formal cause is the shape into which you form these materials, the efficient cause is the agent who builds the structure – you, and the final cause is the end or purpose of the structure – a habitat for Lucky.

Aquinas basically argues here that an object (such as Lucky's house) does not produce itself but is the effect of a previously existing cause (such as you). In turn, this cause did not produce itself but is the effect of a previously existing cause. But this cycle of cause and effect cannot go on indefinitely into the past. To start the sequence, there had to be a First Cause, itself Uncaused, which we call God.

This argument has produced a flurry of criticism. Here are five common objections:

- Aquinas contradicts himself. At the start of the argument, he tells us that all efficient causes owe their existence to previous causes and that no efficient cause produces itself. At the end of the argument, however, he tells us that there is an exception – God, the first efficient cause.
- If God is self-caused, why can't the cosmos be self-caused?
- Aquinas is arbitrary in saying that we cannot go on indefinitely into the past in imagining prior causes. If matter-energy existed indefinitely into the past in some form, we can easily conceive of causes reaching back indefinitely.
- Even if the argument works, it gives us a cold, impersonal, and perhaps material First Cause and not the loving and powerful personal God whom billions worship and pray to.

- Our experience tells us that effects (a century house) often outlast their causes (carpenters, electricians, plumbers, masons, etc.). Thus, even if the argument works, it gives us no assurance that the First Cause exists today.

Pascal's Wager

Blaise Pascal (1623-1662), a French mathematician and scientist, anticipated William James' position that we cannot figure out whether there is or is not a God based on reason. He therefore crafted an argument, called Pascal's Wager, in which he approached the decision about God as a bet. In his *Pensees*, or "Thoughts," a collection of fragmentary writings which editors assembled after he died, he wrote:

> 'God is, or He is not.' But to which side shall we incline? Reason can decide nothing here... What will you wager? According to reason, you can do neither the one thing nor the other; according to reason, you can defend neither of the propositions... (11) Let us weigh the gain and the loss in wagering that God is. Let us estimate these two chances... If you gain, you gain all; if you lose, you lose nothing. Wager, then, without hesitation that He is. (12)
>
> Now, what harm will befall you in taking this side? You will be faithful, honest, humble, grateful, generous, a sincere friend, truthful. Certainly you will not have those poisonous pleasures, glory and luxury; but will you not have others? I will tell you that you will thereby gain in this life, and that, at each step you take on this road, you will see so great certainty of gain, so much nothingness in what you risk, that you will at last recognize that you have wagered for something certain and infinite, for which you have given nothing. (13)

Thus, Pascal sees two wagers: 1) There is a God, and 2) There is no God. You can win or lose each bet. Thus, there are four possible outcomes of wagering:

1. If you bet that there is a God and there is, you win eternal happiness.
2. If you bet that there is a God but there isn't, you lose nothing.
3. If you bet that there is no God and there isn't, you win nothing.
4. If you bet that there isn't a God but there is, you lose eternal happiness.

In essence, Pascal claims that it's in your self-interest to bet on God. It's a win/win strategy. You win if there is a God because you've earned an eternity of happiness. You also win if there is no God because you've lived a virtuous and fulfilling life.

Although Pascal gives us an intriguing proposal, one can raise these objections to it:

- Pascal promotes a faith of expedience, not honest conviction.
  If there is a God, God is likely to be offended by such rank opportunism.
- Pascal assumes that God will reward believers and punish non-believers. But will a good God punish non-believers for eternity? Is a good God capable of everlasting torture? And will a just God punish individuals who found insufficient evidence to support belief in God; it seems odd that God endowed humans with reason if God intended us to abandon it.
- Contrary to Pascal's claim, there is a loss for believers if there is no God. Believers support religious institutions generously; they obediently follow religious authorities at the cost of personal autonomy; and many defer happiness in this life for happiness in an illusory future life.
- Throughout history people have believed in dozens of different gods. The wager offers us no help in identifying which god we should worship. If we choose the wrong God, we're in trouble.
- The wager offers us no help in identifying which of the dozens of religions is the true one ordained by God(s). Again, if we choose the wrong religion, we're in trouble.

The Design Argument

We'll look next at arguably the most popular argument for the existence of God - the argument from design - which derives from Aquinas' fifth argument from the "governance of the world." Philosophers call it the *teleological* argument from the Greek terms for the study of end, purpose, or goal. Let's focus on two figures in history who proposed the design argument. They are William Paley (1743-1805), British clergyman and philosopher, and Thomas Jefferson (1743-1826), principal author of the Declaration of Independence, third president of the United States, and polymath.

Here is the key passage by Paley in his *Natural Theology*:

In crossing a heath, suppose I pitched my foot against a *stone*, and were asked how the stone came to be there. I might possibly answer that for anything I knew to the contrary it had lain there for ever (sic); nor would it, perhaps, be very easy to shew (sic) the absurdity of this answer. But suppose I had found a *watch* upon the ground, and it should be inquired how the watch happened to be in that place. I should hardly think of the answer which I had before given, (namely) that for any thing I knew the watch might have always been there. Yet why should not this answer serve for the watch as well as the stone; why is it not as admissible in the second case as in the first? (The reason is that)...the watch must have had a maker... ...(T)here must have existed, at some time and at some place or other, an artificer or artificers who formed it for the purpose which we find it actually to answer, who comprehended its construction and designed its use... (And) every indication of contrivance, every manifestation of design, which existed in the watch, exists in the works of nature, with the difference on the side of nature of being greater and more, and that in a degree which exceeds all computation. (14)

Next, here is the key passage from Jefferson's letter of April 11, 1823, to John Adams:

...I hold (without appear to revelation) that when we take a view of the universe, in its parts, general or particular, it is impossible for the human mind not to perceive and feel a conviction of design, consummate skill, and indefinite power in every atom of its composition. The movements of the heavenly bodies, so exactly held in their course by the balance of centrifugal and centripetal forces; the structure of our earth itself, with its distribution of lands, waters, and atmosphere; animal and vegetable bodies, examined in all their minutest particles; insects, mere atoms of life, yet as perfectly organized as man or mammoth; the mineral substances, their generation and uses; it is impossible, I say, for the human mind not to believe, that there is in all this, design, cause and effect, up to an ultimate cause, a fabricator of all things from matter and motion, their preserver and regulator while permitted to exist in their present forms, and their regenerator into new and other forms. (15)

Paley's watch gives us the key to the argument. Paley's watch has design. This means that its parts, as to size, shape, composition, and function, are arranged to enable the watch to achieve a purpose, namely, to tell time. Further, the design in the watch is due to an intelligent cause – a watchmaker. Thus, our experience shows us that an object or system with design requires an intelligent cause. Next, as Jefferson points out, we find evidence of design throughout the universe on both the micro-level (insects) and the macro-level (the movements of the heavenly bodies). Since design requires intelligence and the design in nature which Jefferson describes is not the product of human intelligence, there must be a cosmic intelligence, a cosmic architect, which we call God, who is responsible for it.

This is an argument from analogy. An analogy is an inference that if A and B are similar in one respect, they are likely similar in others. Since the watch and the universe possess design, and the design in the watch requires an intelligent (human) cause, then the design in the universe requires an intelligent (non-human) cause. (16)

Despite the continuing popularity of the design argument, like the others, it too has a lot of naysayers. Here are some of the main points of rebuttal:

- We routinely observe cause-and-effect between humans and their products. Chefs produce culinary delights. Protracted alcohol abuse leads to cirrhosis. Failure to study results in poor grades. But it's a stretch to assume that what we observe in our daily lives applies to nature and the cosmos. We observe chefs, heavy drinkers, and lazy students. We don't observe the origin of universes.

- As Darwin discovered, the features of animals, humans included, that we observe today are the result of natural selection over eons of time. Those individuals in a species which had features that promoted survival transmitted them to their offspring, assuring their survival; those who did not inherit such features died off. (17) The idea of an intelligence which steers all this is superfluous.

- Since the design argument derives from Thomas Aquinas' fifth argument from the governance of the world, it is vulnerable to a criticism of that argument. The example of a century house, which we used previously, is appropriate here as well. The house continues to serve its purpose despite the death of the carpenters, electricians, plumbers, and others who built it. Similarly, even if there were a cosmic designer, its products can survive its demise. Thus, the design argument is compatible with the death of God.

- Our environment, near and far, is filled with defects and imperfections. We have deformed babies. Animals, humans included, are afflicted with thousands of sicknesses, diseases, and disorders. Droughts, tsunamis, hurricanes, earthquakes, floods, and tornadoes cause tens of thousands of deaths and injuries every year. Does all this suffering tell us that the cosmic intelligence is flawed – or worse – malicious?
- Even if the design argument works, it doesn't deliver a spiritual designer. Humans, who are physical organisms, produce material products such as watches. Under the principle of analogy, the cosmos, which is a material system, requires only a physical designer.
- Finally, even if the design argument works, it doesn't deliver a creator, one who makes something from nothing. Humans use existing materials to fashion objects with design such as watches. Under the principle of analogy, a cosmic designer uses existing materials to produce a universe with design.

The Argument from Miracles

The term miracle is often used loosely. For instance, if George is routinely late for work, but one day he shows up on time, a boss or a co-worker might say: "George showed up on time today; it's a miracle." But this isn't the type of miracle that religious people speak about. A miracle in religious circles has these characteristics:

- It is a surprising and unexpected event;
- It does not seem to have a rational explanation at the present time;
- It may violate a law of nature;
- It often follows prayer; and
- It is said to be caused by God.

Here are some possible examples of miracles:

1. In defiance of gravitation, a person whose house is being flooded suddenly rises from the floor and flies effortlessly through the air to safety without the aid of a a propulsion device.
2. In violation of all known medical history, a double amputee suddenly grows new limbs.
3. A cancer victim who is terminally ill and on the brink of death fully recovers and lives cancer-free for years.

4.   A young, pregnant woman who sees an accident in which a front wheel of a car comes to rest on a child, single-handedly lifts the car off the child.

Miracles are supported by an argument which draws from science. Science tells us that all events have causes. Religious people say, "Fine, let's apply the principle of causality to miracles" and so we have this argument:

Every event has a cause.
A miracle is an event; thus, a miracle has a cause.
But the cause of a miracle is not a known natural cause.
Therefore, the cause of a miracle is a non-natural cause, namely, God.

Does this argument work? Here are two objections to it:

1.   Did the event called a miracle really occur and, if it did, was it actually a miracle? There is no clear evidence that examples 1 and 2 have ever occurred; indeed, if a person claimed to observe them, we would suspect that lying, trickery, or misperception is at work. Example 3 may be explained by spontaneous remission, misdiagnosis, or response to treatment. Finally, example 4 may be explained by the release of endorphins in the young woman's brain, a common occurrence under stress, which enabled her to block pain and perform this feat of strength.
2.   If prayer preceded the miraculous event, are we sure that prayer caused it? That the event occurred after prayer may be a coincidence. Also, how do we explain that so many prayers go unanswered? Why would God grant one prayer for a miracle but turn a deaf ear to many others?

God and Suffering

Billions of people hold that there is a spiritual and eternal being called God, a being whose power and goodness have no limits, a being who creates and sustains the cosmos. Believers face a serious challenge to this conception of God. The challenge is this:

God is said to have power and goodness without limit. Now, if God has power without limit, God can diminish or abolish suffering, and if God has goodness without limit, God would wish to diminish or abolish suffering.

Yet suffering abounds. Therefore, there must be a limit to God's power, or God's goodness, or both.

This is called the problem of evil or the problem of suffering. Those who attempt to explain how suffering and God can co-exist without contradiction give us what is called a *theodicy*. They face a formidable task. Indeed, many religious skeptics hold that all the proposed justifications of suffering fail and that believers should either abandon their belief in God altogether or radically revise the traditional conception of God.

In this section we will look at the theodicy of John Hick (1922-2012), one of the most respected and influential philosophers of religion in the twentieth century. (18)

Hick recognizes a long-held distinction between two types of evil and he seeks to deal with both. They are *moral evil* and *non-moral evil*. Non-moral evil is also called natural or physical evil. Moral evil is the suffering caused by human beings (e.g., crime). Non-moral evil is the suffering caused by nature (e.g., tsunamis). Hick gives us four arguments to justify suffering.

1. *Freedom*. God has conferred upon humankind the precious gift of free will. This elevates our status in the hierarchy of creation because it gives us autonomy, the power to direct our own lives, which no other species enjoys. Hick writes:

> To be a person is to be a finite center of freedom, a (relatively) free and self-directing agent responsible for one's own decisions. This involves being free to act wrongly as well as to act rightly. (19)

With freedom we have the power to choose good – to tell the truth, to be kind, to respect the rights of others, to keep our promises, and to deal with conflicts peacefully; and we have the power to choose evil – to tell a lie, to be cruel, to violate the rights of others, to break our promises, and to deal with conflicts violently. When people freely choose good, **they** deserve our praise. And when they freely choose evil, **they** - *not God* - deserve our blame.

2. *Soul-Making*. Hick says that suffering has an important purpose. It prompts people to grow in virtue and merit salvation. The world, he observes, is not a "paradise" with "a maximum of pleasure and a minimum of pain," but instead:

...a place of 'soul-making' in which free beings grappling with the tasks and challenges of their existence in a common environment, may become 'children of God' and 'heirs of eternal life. (20)

To see Hick's point, consider two examples:

* Michael, an impudent person and a braggart, has too much to drink at a tavern. Impaired, he drives home but swerves left of center, causing a horrific accident, which results in the deaths of the parents of three young children. Michael is seriously injured but survives after multiple surgeries and rehabilitation. As time passes, Michael comes to value his doctors, nurses, and therapists, he pledges to help the surviving children for the rest of his life, and he speaks to groups about the dangers of drinking and driving. Through this tragedy Michael has become a better person. He has learned humility, compassion, and accountability. Suffering – his and others – set the stage for growth in virtue.

* An earthquake beneath the Indian Ocean causes a tidal wave hundreds of miles wide which drowns over 100,000 people and destroys billions of dollars of property in a dozen countries. In the aftermath of the tsunami, millions of people around the world rally around the survivors with donations of money and goods to help them rebuild their lives. Thousands of volunteers from around the world descend on the region to help in person. The tragedy has unified a divided world in sympathy and compassion for the victims. Here, again, suffering set the stage for growth in virtue.

3. *Culpable Incompetence.* Hick attributes much of the suffering in the world to a lack of knowledge or skills - incompetence - for which human beings are justifiably to blame - culpable. All of us are incompetent in many areas. For instance, I am incompetent in theoretical physics, auto repair, and cardiac bypass surgery. (Indeed, the list could run for pages!) But should I be blamed for this lack of knowledge and skill in domains in which I have not been educated and in which I claim no expertise? Of course not. But if I, a philosopher, do not know the difference between Groucho Marx and Karl Marx, I should be fired on the spot. In this case I would lack knowledge that I should have, given my education and my

profession. Hick's argument from culpable incompetence affirms that there is a parallel between me and the human community. Just as I lack knowledge about Karl Marx that I should have, the human community lacks knowledge about many things that it should have. Take cancer. Although we have invested a lot in cancer research which has reduced suffering, we have spent only a fraction of what we could have spent. For decades cancer was not a high priority. As a result, there are still tens of millions of cancer victims worldwide every year. The failure of the human community to dedicate itself aggressively to cancer research needlessly perpetuates suffering and for this the human community – not God – should be blamed. (21)

4. *The Impossibility of Divine Intervention.* People often pray to God to intervene to prevent or reduce suffering. So, why doesn't God do so? Hick's answer is that continuing intervention by God to block suffering in every case is impossible. His reasoning is that humans need a uniform, stable environment in which to live. If God were to intervene on the planet in all instances to impede suffering, the laws of nature would collapse. He writes:

> ...(N)o one could ever injure anyone else; the murderer's knife would turn to paper or his bullets to thin air; the bank safe, robbed of a million dollars, would miraculously become filled with another million dollars...; fraud, deceit, conspiracy, and treason would somehow always leave the fabric of society undamaged... (T)he mountain climber, steeplejack, or playing child falling from a height would float unharmed to the ground; the reckless driver would never meet with disaster... (N)ature would have to work by 'special providences' instead of running according to general laws... (S)ometimes gravity would operate, sometimes not... In eliminating the problems and hardships of an objective environment, with its own laws, life would become like a dream in which, delightfully but aimlessly, we would float and drift at ease. (22)

What's more, Hick tells us, a world in which God constantly intervenes would be a world where right and wrong would disappear as live options because we could not possibly do wrong. If we intended to harm another person, for instance, we would fail. Our intention could never be realized because God wouldn't permit it. Humans would be compelled by God always to choose good and never to choose evil; thus, human free will would be impossible. Further, Hick adds, where there is "no danger or difficulty," virtues such as courage would be pointless. Soul-making could not possibly occur.

Does Hick's theodicy exonerate the all-powerful and all-good God of tradition? You make the call after thinking about the following criticisms:

- Hick emphasizes that human freedom enables us to do good and evil. For starters, is it possible for God to remain all-powerful if humans possess power to direct their own lives? Next, in the wake of the Holocaust, terrorism, murder, rape, and child molesting, is free will such a precious gift? Finally, even if God endowed us with free will, couldn't God have given us a stronger disposition to do the good than we have? And, even if God endowed us with free will, God is still responsible for natural evil (diseases, tornadoes, hurricanes, tsunamis, etc.).

- On soul-making, it is true that many instances of suffering produce benefits. However, on an objective cost-benefit analysis, does the benefit justify the cost? If an earthquake destroys a school and kills many of the faculty, staff, and students, and a new, state-of-the-art building replaces it, with smaller classes and enhanced learning, should we celebrate? Or, say a young police officer is shot to death on duty. The officer's death moves family and friends to establish a college scholarship in his name which helps a small number of students pay part of the expenses of their education every year. Does the benefit to the students justify and offset the death of the officer? Further, many instances of suffering produce no apparent benefit. If a crib death sends a mother into depression, from which she never recovers, where is the benefit? One might respond that crib deaths prompted safety improvements through redesign. But does it take deaths to produce improvements? Couldn't an injury to a baby prompt them? (23)

- On culpable incompetence, Hick observes that humans often drag their feet when faced with the causes of suffering. Two points are relevant. If humans are chronically lazy and tend to procrastinate when faced with a problem such as cancer, shouldn't the creator receive at least some of the blame? And, even if suffering triggers soul-making, the challenge which we confront is overwhelming. Do we need to be afflicted by thousands of illnesses and diseases to promote soul-making? Wouldn't a dozen or so serve the purpose adequately?

- Hick's argument about divine intervention has merit. Yet one point should be made. Occasional interventions to prevent calamities would not seem to upset the stable environment which Hick says we need to live. For instance, it seems that an all-powerful God could have seen to it that Hitler was never born (or, if born, never rose to power) without undermining the laws of nature and destabilizing the environment. This would have saved millions of lives.

To conclude this discussion, let's mention briefly one further explanation of suffering that is popular among some followers of Christianity, Islam, and Judaism. Some claim that there is a malicious being called Satan or the Devil who roams the earth, confronts people with temptation, and lures them to sin. According to this view, Satan is so effective that millions succumb to his influence. They rape, murder, steal, lie, commit adultery, and perform other deeds which exacerbate suffering across the world. One who harbors this belief faces these challenges: 1) The existence of Satan must be proven; it may not simply be taken on faith; 2) Belief in Satan and belief in an all-powerful and all-good God must be shown to be compatible. At first glance, this does not seem to be the case. If Satan is beyond God's control, it would seem that God's power has limits; if Satan is not beyond God's control, it would seem that God's goodness has limits. Today, perhaps because of these challenges, most people, believers and non-believers alike, view Satan not as an actual being but instead as a symbol of humanity's lower nature.

Footnotes:

1. It can be objected that Deism is an exception. Deism was a "religion of reason" popular in Europe and America in the 1700s. However, since Deists, such as Jefferson, rejected faith as the basis of belief, it is doubtful that Deism qualifies as a religion in the way that the belief systems listed here do.

2. *Webster's Tenth New Collegiate Dictionary*, p. 418.

3. *The End of Faith*, W. W. Norton & Co., 2004, 2005, p. 19. Also, in the following passage, Mitchell Stephens highlights the resistance of many religious people to the demand of science for proof:

    For science's methods are clearly troublesome for religion. The devout, to begin with, are not wont to view their precepts merely as a proposition to be controverted or confirmed. The orthodox, as a rule, are used to arguments being settled by authority, not experiment. The hope belief offers does not always stand up well to observation and experience: life sometimes works out okay; sometimes it doesn't. Faith, particularly of the "certain-because-impossible" variety, and reason have long been tussling. Miracles are notoriously miserly with evidence. Revelation does not lend itself to experimental verification. And the mystical, by its nature, fails to produce facts. *Imagine There's No Heaven*, Palgrave Macmillan, 2014, p. 86.

4. *Contemporary Review*, 1877.

5. For a discussion of harm caused by religion in history, see James A. Haught, *Holy Horrors: An Illustrated History of Religious Murder and Madness*, Prometheus Books, 1990, and for a discussion of harm caused by religion in today's world, see Sam Harris, *The End of Faith*, W. W. Norton & Co., 2004, 2005.

6. *New World*, June 1886. James originally titled this "The Will to Believe" but he later conceded that he should have titled it "The Right to Believe." See *The Letters of William James*, Volume 2, Longmans, Green & Company, 1920, p. 207.

7. From Thomas A. Shipka and Arthur J. Minton, *Philosophy: Paradox and Discovery*, Fifth Edition, McGraw-Hill, 2004, p. 27.

8. Rene Descartes, *Meditations and Other Metaphysical Writings*, Translated with an Introduction by Desmond M. Clarke, Penguin Books, 2000, p. 38. It was originally published in 1641 in Latin. Subsequent quotes from the *Meditations* in this chapter and Chapter 3 are taken from this source. The full title of the *Meditations* is *Meditations on the First Philosophy in which God's existence and the distinction between the human soul and the body are demonstrated*.

9. *Ibid.*, p. 53.

10. From *Summa Theologica* in *The Basic Writings of St. Thomas Aquinas*, Volume One, Question 2, Article 3, Edited and Annotated, with an Introduction, by Anton C. Pegis, Random House, 1945, p. 23.

11. Pascal, *Pensees*, in *Great Books of the Western World*, Volume 33, Encyclopedia Britannica, 1952, p. 214.

12. *Ibid.*, p. 215.

13. *Ibid.*, p. 216.

14. William Paley, *Natural Theology*, General Books, 2010, p. 3, p. 8.

15. Thomas Jefferson, *The Life and Selected Writings of Thomas Jefferson*, Edited by Adrienne Koch and William Peden, The Modern Library, 1944, pp. 706-707.

16. Advocacy for the design argument is not the only bond between Paley and Jefferson. Paley enthusiastically supported the American Revolution. Beyond this, they were worlds apart. Paley was a Christian minister and apologist while Jefferson, a Deist, abandoned traditional religion.

17. In the *Origin of Species*, Darwin wrote:

    As many more individuals of each species are born than can possibly survive; and as, consequently, there is a frequently recurring struggle for existence, it follows that any being, if it vary however slightly in any manner profitable to itself, under the complex and sometimes varying conditions of life, will have a better chance of surviving, and thus be naturally selected. From the strong principle of inheritance, any selected variety will tend to propagate its new and modified form.

    Charles Darwin, *The Origin of Species and the Descent of Man*, The Modern Library, n.d., p. 13.

18. See John Hick, *Philosophy of Religion*, Fourth Edition, Prentice Hall, 1990.

19. *Ibid.*, p. 40.

20. *Ibid.*, p. 46.

21. Hick gives more attention to culpable incompetence in the 1963 edition of *Philosophy of Religion* than in later editions, especially the 1990 edition. Nevertheless, in all editions he makes the point that the line between moral and natural evil blurs in practice because action or inaction by humans, for which we can often be blamed, perpetuates a great deal of evil initially caused by nature.

22. Hick, *Ibid.*, p. 46.

23. Hick essentially admits this point. He says that only belief in an afterlife where soul-making continues enables us to make sense of suffering in this life which fails to promote soul-making. *Philosophy of Religion*, p. 47.

Recommendations for Further Study:

1. John Hick, *Philosophy of Religion*, Prentice-Hall, Inc., Fourth Edition, 1990.

2. John Hick, *An Interpretation of Religion*, Yale, 1989.

3. Harold S. Kushner, *When Bad Things Happen to Good People*, Schocken Books, 1981.

4. Ronald H. Nash, *Faith & Reason: Searching for a Rational Faith*, Zondervan, 1988.

5. Kenneth Miller, *Finding Darwin's God*, HarperCollins, 1999.

6. John F. Haught, *God After Darwin*, Westview, 2008.

7. C. S. Lewis, *Miracles: A Preliminary Study*, Macmillan, 1947.

8. C. S. Lewis, *The Problem of Pain*, HarperOne, 2001.

9. Paul Kurtz, *Transcendental Temptation*, Prometheus Books, 1986.

10. Paul Kurtz, *In Defense of Secular Humanism*, Prometheus Books, 1983.

11. Richard Dawkins, *The Blind Watchmaker*, Norton, 1986.

12. Richard Dawkins, *The God Delusion*, Houghton Mifflin, 2006.

13. James A. Haught, *Holy Horrors: An Illustrated History of Religious Murder and Madness*, Prometheus Books, 1990.

14. James A. Haught, *2000 Years of Disbelief: Famous People with the Courage to Doubt*, Prometheus Books, 1996.

15. Sam Harris, *The End of Faith*, 2004.

16. Sam Harris, *Letter to a Christian Nation*, Knopf, 2007.

17. Sam Harris, *Waking Up: A Guide to Spirituality Without Religion*, Simon & Schuster, 2014.

18. Christopher Hitchens, *god is not Great*, Hachette Book Group, 2007.

19. Daniel Dennett, *Breaking the Spell: Religion as a Natural Phenomenon*, Viking, 2006.

20. Mike David, *The Atheist's Introduction to the New Testament: How the Bible Undermines the Basic Teachings of Christianity*, Outskirts Press, 2008.

21. Philip Kitcher, *Life After Faith: The Case for Secular Humanism*, Yale University Press, 2014.

22. Chris Hedges, *American Fascists*, Free Press, 2006.

23. Chris Hedges, *I Don't Believe in Atheists*, Free Press, 2008.

24. John F. Haught, *The New Atheism*, Westminster John Knox, 2008.

25. David J. Wolpe, *Why Faith Matters*, HarperOne, 2008.

26. Brian J. Alters and Sandra M. Alters, *Defending Evolution*, Jones and Bartlett, 2001.

27. Guy P. Harrison, *50 reasons people give for believing in a god*, Prometheus Books, 2008.

28. Guy P. Harrison, *50 simple questions for every Christian*, Prometheus Books, 2013.

29. John W. Loftus, *The Outsider Test for Religion: How to Know Which Religion Is True*, Prometheus Books, 2013.

30. Jerry DeWitt with Ethan Brown, *Hope After Faith: An Ex-Pastor's Journey from Belief to Atheism*, Da Capo Press, 2013.

31. Mitchell Stephens, *Imagine There's No Heaven: How Atheism Helped Create the Modern World*, Palgrave Macmillan, 2014.

32. Michael Ruse, *Science and Spirituality: Making Room for Faith in the Age of Science*, Cambridge University Press, 2010.

33. Jerry A. Coyne, *Faith versus Fact: Why Science and Religion are Incompatible*, Viking, 2015.

34. Greta Christina, *Coming Out Atheist: How to Do It, How to Help Each Other, and Why*, Pitchstone Publishing, 2014.

35. Sarah Sentilles, *Breaking Up With God*, HarperOne, 2011.

36. Edward O. Wilson, *The Meaning of Human Existence*, Liveright, 2014, especially Chapter 13, Religion, pp. 147-158.

37. Susan Jacoby, *Freethinkers: A History of American Secularism*, Metropolitan Books, 2004.

38. Susan Jacoby, *The Great Agnostic: Robert Ingersoll and American Freethought*, Yale University Press, 2013.

39. Bernard Lewis, *Islam and the West*, Oxford University Press, 1993.

40. Michael Shermer, *Heavens on Earth: The Scientific Search for the Afterlife, Immortality, and Utopia*, Henry Holt and Company, 2018.

41. Bill Zuersher, *Seeing through Christianity: A Critique of Beliefs and Evidence*, Xlibris, 2014.

42. Dan Gilgoff, *The Jesus Machine*, St. Martin's Press, 2007.

43. Phil Zuckerman, *Living the Secular Life*, 2014.

44. Greg Epstein, *Good Without God: What a Billion Non-Religious People Do Believe*, William Morrow, 2009.

45. Susan Jacoby, *Strange Gods: A Secular History of Conversions*, Pantheon Books, 2016.

46. Bart D. Ehrman, *Misquoting Jesus: The Story Behind Who Changed the Bible and Why*, Harper One, 2005.

47. Bart D. Ehrman, *Jesus Before the Gospels*, Harper One, 2016.

48. Jon Mills, *Inventing God: Psychology of Belief and the Rise of Secular Spirituality*, Routledge, 2017.

49. Raymond D. Bradley, *God's Gravediggers: Why No Deity Exists*, Ockham Publishing, 2015.

Readings: Religion

Faith

Tom Shipka (2015)

Religious people often refer to faith as a precious gift from God which they cherish. (1) But what exactly is this gift called faith? And is it really precious? According to *Webster's* dictionary, faith is "firm belief in something for which there is no proof." (2) By contrast, knowledge is belief in something for which there is proof. For instance, if you believe in the virgin birth and the resurrection of Jesus, or heaven and hell, or reincarnation, or divine authorship of a religious scripture, you have faith, and if you believe that water boils at 212 degrees Fahrenheit, that smoking cigarettes is harmful to a person, and that regular exercise is helpful to a person, you have knowledge. (To possess knowledge, however, means not only that you hold a belief that is true but that you understand why it is true; thus, knowledge is true, justified belief. If you hold a belief that is true but you do not understand why it is true, you have faith, not knowledge.) Faith is the foundation of religion while reason and science are the foundation of knowledge.

Having said this, let's acknowledge, however, that faith does play a role in science. A scientist often embraces a belief without proof tentatively as a hypothesis, sometimes based on a mere hunch, to test whether it is supported by evidence. If the hypothesis turns out to be confirmed by the evidence, he or she then publishes the results of the research to peers so that they can evaluate the validity of the test and duplicate its findings. This type of provisional "faith" is markedly different from that exhibited in religion where believers typically embrace a belief as a certainty with no intent (or even possibility) to test it as scientists do.

While faith is held in high regard by tens of millions of Americans, the fact is that once we endorse faith, once we authorize people to believe without proof, we open a Pandora's Box, (3) for faith takes people down many different paths. On the one hand, there are benign paths where the faithful perform socially beneficial acts. They volunteer at a food bank, give to a charity, rescue abandoned and abused animals, or donate an organ. On the other hand, there are not so benign paths where the faithful perform socially harmful acts such as the following (4):

*   Some Christians, following a passage in the Epistle of James (5:14), rely exclusively on prayer and never on doctors, to heal the sick. This results

in the avoidable death of hundreds, if not thousands, in the United States every year, especially children;

* Some Christians, believing that God directs them to stop abortions at any cost, murder medical staff, patients, and volunteers at women's clinics; (5)
* Some Muslims, following passages in the Qur'an (Sura 4:76 and Sura 8:12) and the Hadith (Muslim 1:20), the teachings and deeds attributed to the prophet Muhammed, seek to murder non-Muslims - infidels - even at the cost of their own lives, resulting in violent attacks around the world; (6) and
* In many majority-Muslim nations, Sharia, a legal system based on the Qur'an and the Hadith, provides that the rape of a woman can be proven only by admission of the rapist or the testimony of four male witnesses. (Needless to say, if they witnessed the rape, they were complicit in it.) The victim's testimony is inadmissible. (7)

As bad as these expressions of faith are, the situation could be worse. This is because the faithful often cherry-pick scriptures and religious teachings. For instance, if Christians followed the Bible to the letter,

* They would own slaves (Leviticus 25:44-46, Ephesians 6:5); (8)
* They would murder homosexuals (Leviticus 20:13), unruly children (Exodus 21:15, Exodus 21:17), non-virgin brides (Deuteronomy 22:20-21), and adulterers (Deuteronomy 22:22-24); (9) and
* They would condemn divorce (Mark 10:2-12, Luke 16:18) and tattoos (Leviticus 19:28). (10)

So, what is the lesson here? It's the same lesson taught in the 19th century by W.K. Clifford, a British mathematician. (11) Recognizing that our beliefs translate into actions which can cause harm to ourselves and others, Clifford insisted that we acquire proof – what he called "sufficient evidence" – before we embrace and act upon a belief. For Clifford, this requires the path of reason and science, not the path of faith. In essence, Clifford warns that the path of faith is a dead end – literally and figuratively.

I have little hope that a majority of humans near or far will heed Clifford's warning any time soon. Those who believe that they speak and act on the commands of Christianity's God or Islam's Allah or some other god, or their messenger, will obey those commands at any cost. The proof that reason demands is irrelevant to them.

1. Many believers insist that faith in divine justice in the hereafter is essential to a moral life on earth. On this issue, see Phil Zuckerman, *Society without God: What the Least Religious Nations Can Tell Us About Contentment*, New York University Press, 2008. This study of Denmark and Sweden, where most people are atheist or agnostic, shows that violent crime is very low, altruistic behavior is very high, and overall societal health is superior to religious nations such as the United States.

2. *Webster's Tenth New Collegiate Dictionary*, p. 418.

3. According to an ancient Greek myth, the gods bestowed gifts upon the beautiful Pandora in a box but instructed her never to open it. When her curiosity won out, however, she opened the box only to discover to her shock that she unleashed illnesses and hardships galore upon the human race.

4. The focus here is contemporary faith-based beliefs among Christians and Muslims. Poignant examples are available from the past, including the Crusades, the Inquisition, witch hunts, persecution of Jews by Christians in Europe, human sacrifice in South America, etc.

5. Other examples from Christianity include these. Some Christians, following Proverbs 22:15, beat their children, and in many Christian families, following Ephesians 5:22-24, wives are subservient to their husbands;

6. The Qur'an says: "I will cast terror into the hearts of those who disbelieve. Therefore strike off their heads and strike off every fingertip of them" (Sura 8:12) and "The true believers fight for the cause of God, but the infidels fight for the devil. Fight then against the friends of Satan." (Sura 4:76) Also, the Hadith says: "The Messenger of Allah said: I have been commanded to fight against people so long as they do not declare that there is no God but Allah." (Muslim 1:30)

7. Further, Sharia also provides that a man determined to be a rapist need only pay his victim a fee and, remarkably, that a woman whose claim of rape is not corroborated by the rapist or four witnesses is subject to punishment as a fornicator or adulterer. Other examples from Islam include the following: In many majority-Muslim nations, Sharia forbids criticism of Islam, and calls for jail, torture, or death for those deemed apostates or heretics; Saudi Arabia, a wealthy Muslim nation, promotes Wahhabism, an extreme form of Islam, and sponsors madrassas around the world, "schools," which often exclude girls and where the curriculum consists mainly of memorizing the Qur'an and studying Islam; and violence periodically breaks out in the Middle East between Sunni and Shia Muslims who consider one another heretics.

8. The Qur'an also permits the owning of slaves. See Sura 5:89 and Sura 23:1.

9.   Thus, the Christian county official in Kentucky who refused to sign marriage permits for same-sex couples in 2015 violated Biblical commands by doing too little.

10. Examples of faith-based nonsense in other countries include these: In at least three nations in Africa – Sierra Leone, Liberia, and Guinea – the spread of Ebola is fueled by family members and friends washing and dressing the body of the deceased and mourners at the funeral touching it to make sure that the dead don't return to haunt the living; in India, where believers take their own religion as superior to others, violence regularly breaks out among Hindus, Christians, and Muslims; and following Hindu tradition, some women whose husbands die choose to immolate themselves on their husband's funeral pyre even if they have young children.

11. See W.K. Clifford, "The Ethics of Belief," *Contemporary Review*, 1877.

Guy P. Harrison on Religion

Tom Shipka (2012)

After years of interviewing hundreds of believers of more than a dozen religions around the world, Guy P. Harrison has written a book entitled *50 reasons people give for believing in a god* (1) in which he strives to be a kinder and gentler religious skeptic than the so-called "new atheists." (2) Harrison writes:

> This (book) is a respectful reply to the friendly people around the world who shared with me their reasons for believing... My fifty replies to common justifications for belief can be read as friendly chats designed to do nothing more than stimulate critical thinking. (p. 14)

Let's take a look at three of the reasons which believers gave Harrison and his replies.

Firstly, believers say, it is *obvious* that god exists. After all, god is everywhere, god made everything, god answers prayers, and god runs the universe. But how can god's existence be so obvious, Harrison asks, when you consider that between 500 million and 750 million people on our planet are non-believers and that 93% of the elite scientists in the United States are non-believers? And how do you explain that beliefs about god in the two largest religions – Christianity and Islam – contradict one another? Christians insist that Jesus is god and the Bible is god's revelation while Muslims insist that Jesus is not god and the Qur'an is god's revelation. Further, he notes, half the world's population recognizes neither Jesus nor Allah! (pp. 17-22)

Secondly, believers claim that "Society would fall apart without religion." (p. 295) If this is true, Harrison replies, then we would expect to find the least religious nations to be "bastions of crime, poverty and disease" and the most religious ones to be "models of societal health" but this isn't the case. He cites reports by the United Nations and research by social scientists which show that indicators of societal health are highest in the least religious nations and lowest in the most religious ones. The most secular nations – Sweden, Norway, Australia, the Netherlands, and Canada – lead the world in life expectancy, adult literacy, per-capita income, educational attainment, and the status of women, and have the lowest rates of homicides, AIDS, and HIV. By contrast, the worst performing nations on these same indicators are among the most religious ones. (pp. 295-301)

Thirdly, believers say that the age of their religion is evidence of its merit. "A lie or a mistake," they declare, "could not have endured for so long." (p. 303) The problem with this justification, Harrison argues, is that *many* religions are old and *many* are not. If age is pivotal, he notes, we should all be Hindus because Hinduism, a polytheistic religion, is at least 6,000 years old, and we should abandon "relatively young religions" such as Christianity, Islam, Mormonism, and Scientology. (pp. 303-307)

During his travels and interviews, Harrison made three important discoveries. The first is that, when it comes to religion, comparison shopping is virtually non-existent. Nearly all believers follow the religion of their parents or their geographical region. The second is that most followers of a given religion have little or no knowledge of other religions. And the third is that most believers have little interest in formulating or evaluating arguments about god or religion because they rely on faith – belief without proof.

It remains to be seen whether Harrison's *50 reasons* will spur the self-assessment and critical thinking that he hopes for in religious circles. That aside, the book is a helpful and informative guide to the deeply felt convictions of believers around the world and one observer's measured response to them.

1. Prometheus Books, 2008, p. 14. Future references to this book are by page number.
2. The "new atheists" include Sam Harris, Richard Dawkins, Daniel Dennett, and the late Christopher Hitchens. Many readers, both religious and non-religious, have judged their work to be arrogant, dismissive, and insulting. For instance, see John F. Haught, *God and the New Atheism*, Westminister John Knox Press, 2008, and Chris Hedges, *I Don't Believe in Atheists*, Free Press, 2008.

Science and Intercessory Prayer – The STEP Study

Tom Shipka (2006)

There are several types of prayer. One type praises God (glorification), another thanks God (gratitude), and yet another requests God's help (petitionary). One may request God's help for oneself or for others. Seeking God's help for others is called intercessory prayer. The most comprehensive study of intercessory prayer ever done was published recently in the March 30, 2006, online edition of *The American Heart Journal*. It is titled the *Study of the Therapeutic Effects of Intercessory Prayer*, or STEP. STEP was supported by a $2.4 million grant from the John Templeton Foundation whose mission is to build bridges between science and religion, and it was directed by Dr. Herbert Benson, a cardiologist on the staff of the Harvard University Medical School and Beth Israel Hospital in Boston. At Beth Israel Dr. Benson directs the Mind-Body Institute. He first came to prominent in 1975 with the publication of a book entitled *Relaxation Response* which promoted relaxation techniques such as meditation to promote good mental and physical health and he is one of the central figures in contemporary medicine who recommends prayer as a component of a religious person's healing.

The STEP study involved 1,802 patients undergoing coronary bypass surgery in six different hospitals. STEP was designed "to study the effect of intercessory prayer (on these patients) and whether (their) knowledge that (they were) receiving prayer made a difference... Results were measured in terms of the number of medical complications encountered by each patient after surgery." (Gregory Lamb, Online Edition, *Christian Science Monitor*, April 3, 2006) The patients were divided into three groups. One group was prayed for and knew that it was prayed for; a second group was prayed for but was told that it might or might not be prayed for; and a third group – the control group – was not prayed for but was told that it might or might not be prayed for. Prayers were offered by Silent Unity, a Protestant prayer ministry in Kansas City, Missouri; the Community of Teresian Carmelites in Worcester, Massachusetts; and the congregation of St. Paul's Monastery in St. Paul, Minnesota. Those offering prayers were permitted to craft their own prayers but all prayers were required to request "a successful surgery with a quick, healthy recovery and no complications." Prayers began the night before surgery and continued daily for two weeks after surgery. Researchers monitored patients for a month after surgery.

And what were the results? The study showed that "intercessory prayer...had no effect on recovery from bypass surgery." (David G. Myers, *Arm Twisting with the Almighty*, Online Edition, *Science & Theology News*, June 27, 2006) Oddly, the group which knew that it was being prayed for had a higher rate of post-surgical complications than the other two groups. The authors of the study hypothesize that the patients who knew that they were being prayed for may have suffered additional anxiety based on their assumption that they received prayers because their condition was especially serious. (Lamb, *Ibid.*)

The STEP study is particularly important because it is the most rigorous and comprehensive study of the link between intercessory prayer and health ever conducted, it was carefully designed to correct for flaws in previous research on the subject (Lamb, *Ibid.*), and, given the reputation of its director, Dr. Benson, the conclusion that intercessory prayer is ineffective cannot be attributed to investigator bias.

In the wake of the STEP study, here's my advice. If you're going to have surgery soon and your relatives and friends offer to pray for you, feel free to accept the offer, but in the meanwhile, make sure that your surgeon is board-certified and that your hospital is accredited.

CHAPTER 3
Knowledge

An Overview

Belief and Knowledge

Consider the following statements (1):

* The Philadelphia Eagles beat the New England Patriots in Super Bowl LII.
* Smoking four packs of cigarettes a day promotes good health and a long life.
* A smerlala is a mix of lalooza and zak.

If you support one of these statements, we say that you hold a *belief*. For instance, if you support the first one, it is your belief (or you *believe*) that "The Philadelphia Eagles beat the New England Patriots in Super Bowl LII." Since each of the three statements is true, false, or meaningless, your belief, in turn, is true (accurate, correct, sound, justified, reliable), false (inaccurate, incorrect, unsound, unjustified, unreliable), or meaningless (unintelligible, makes no sense). Furthermore, if your belief is *true* and you can show why it is true, that is, you can justify it, we say that you have *knowledge*. Thus, *knowledge is true, justified belief.* If you accept the invitation of this book to take a fresh look at your beliefs, you try to figure out if a given belief of yours rises to the level of knowledge. This is not easy. As was explained previously, we tend to form and retain beliefs which meet the PASS criteria: *popularity* – most people whom we know or know about believe them; *age* – they were handed down for generations; *socialization* – we were taught them as we grew up or later on; and *satisfaction* – we find them satisfying, consoling, fulfilling. Just because a belief meets the PASS test, however, is no guarantee that it is true. (2)

In this chapter, we'll discuss how we gain knowledge. To help us do so, we will focus first on an influential philosopher – Descartes – whom we met in Chapter 2: Religion.

Descartes: An Exposition

Late in his life Rene Descartes (1596-1650), French philosopher and mathematician, undertook a project which was prompted by the upsurge of modern science - The Scientific Revolution - through legendary figures including Copernicus (1473-1543), Galileo (1564-1642), Bacon (1561-1626), Harvey (1578-1657), Hobbes (1588-1679), and Newton (1642-1727). Copernicus and Galileo theorized that the sun, not the earth, is the center of the universe; Bacon established the fact-based method of modern science; Harvey discovered that the heart pumps blood through the body and that the structure of humans is remarkably similar to other animals; Hobbes taught that humans are material beings, not spiritual ones; and Newton discovered the universal law of gravitation and the three laws of motion which clinched the case for Copernicus. Traditional beliefs, religious ones among them, were now on the defensive. The Church's punishment of Galileo in the ecclesiastical court called the Inquisition failed to stem the tide. Enter Descartes.

Descartes believed that he could demonstrate that the march of science posed no threat to cherished traditional beliefs such as God and the soul. To do this, he undertook a "once in a lifetime" project - to "seriously and freely" reevaluate all of his beliefs and to retain only those that are "certain and indubitable." (3) He pledged to set aside all beliefs subject to any doubt as if they are "clearly false." (4) Does this require him to evaluate his myriad beliefs one by one? No, he says...

> ...(T)hey need not be reviewed individually, for that would be an infinite task; as soon as the foundations are undermined everything built on them collapses of its own accord, and therefore I will challenge directly all the first principles on which everything I formerly believed rests. (5)

And what is the "foundation" of his beliefs? Here is his answer:

> Everything that I accepted as being most true up to now I acquired
> from the senses or through the senses. However, I have occasionally
> found that they deceive me, and it is prudent never to trust those
> who have deceived us, even if only once. (6)

He goes on the say, as he reflects on his sense experience, that he cannot distinguish his experience while dreaming from his experience while awake. Further, he argues, even if there is "a powerful and cunning" deceiver which causes him to believe in a non-existent physical world, including his own body, he must exist to be deceived. Exist as what? As "a thinking being, that is, a mind, soul, intellect or reason..."

After establishing his own existence as a thinking being, Descartes uses two versions of the ontological argument to prove the existence of God, as we saw in Chapter 2: Religion. But how about the physical world? Early on, he said that he could not trust his senses, through which he grasps physical things, and therefore he could not be certain that there is a physical world. Nevertheless, he reports that he cannot rid himself of ideas of physical things. If God had so strongly disposed him to entertain these ideas but there is no physical world, this would make God, a perfect being, a deceiver, which is impossible.

Descartes writes:

> But God is not a deceiver; it is perfectly obvious, therefore, that he does
> not send these ideas to me directly from himself. Nor does he send them
> indirectly by means of some creature which contains the intentional real-
> ity of the ideas, not formally but only eminently. He obviously gave me no
> faculty to recognize such an arrangement; on the contrary, he gave me a
> strong tendency to believe that these ideas are emitted by physical things.
> Therefore, physical things exist. (7)

What Descartes gives us is *Rationalism*, the position that reason (not the senses, as the *Empiricists* claim) is the path to knowledge, and *dualism*, the position that there are two levels of reality, physical and non-physical, not one. On both counts he buffers the growing influence of the Scientific Revolution. In essence, he says to his contemporaries:

> *Fear not the rise of science and its preoccupation with the physical. Scientists know that what they study is real and not illusory because God guarantees it and because God has given them souls that are the seat of thought.*

Descartes surely felt that his project of methodical doubt was a noble attempt to reconcile religion and science, to show the reliance of science on traditional religious beliefs, and to preserve these beliefs as science gained more and more traction in Western civilization. If Descartes expected applause from the Church, however, he was disappointed. Indeed, the Church placed his *Meditations* and other writings on the *Index Librorum Prohibitorum*, a list of books the Church forbad Christians from reading. Why was the Church so incensed? Historically the Church saw itself as the bridge to truth, as the infallible guide to God's revelation. It expected faith and obedience. Now, suddenly, Descartes charts a new path to truth, one based on reason, skepticism, and self-reliance, not submission to authority. This was a game changer and the Church recognized it.

Descartes: An Assessment

How should we size up Descartes? Here are five points to think about:

1. Descartes' worry about the reliability of sense experience is widely shared and documented in contemporary psychological research. There are pitfalls when we use our sensory organs - sight, hearing, smell, taste, and touch - which we need to understand and guard against. (8) On the other hand, Descartes overreacts to the problem when he attempts to abandon sense experience and what it conveys to us. The fact is that reason cannot function without the senses because the senses furnish the fuel which reason needs to carry out its functions. Consider what you've done in the past few minutes. Your eyes perused the words on each page and sent sensory data to your brain which triggered your thinking - interpreting, questioning, understanding, evaluating, and judging - about his arguments. Neither you, nor I, nor Descartes can abandon sense experience or relegate it to a marginal

role in knowing. Indeed, he virtually concedes this in the *Meditations* when he admits, repeatedly, that try as he might, he cannot rid himself of sensory impressions. (9)

2. Soon after Descartes launches his reappraisal of his beliefs, he establishes certainty as the only acceptable standard for retention of a belief. This is both arbitrary and counter-productive. Although there may be beliefs that we can establish as a certainty, tautologies among them (e.g., 2+2=4, A bachelor is an unmarried man.), the great bulk of our knowledge is highly probable, not certain.

    For instance, I hold these beliefs:

    - My car will slow down and stop as I depress the brake,
    - An elevator in a multi-story building will take me safely to the floor that I want, and
    - The food that I order in a restaurant won't make me sick.

    Am I certain of these beliefs? No. I recognize that certainty is typically out of reach and that a high level of probability is sufficient for purposes of action. Moreover, requiring certainty before one acts is not only impractical but dangerous. If we had failed to act on beliefs until we were certain of them, we would have denied billions of people past and present the benefits of highly probable beliefs about agriculture, nutrition, germs, disease, medicines, energy, chemicals, construction, transportation, surgery, exercise, hygiene, and countless other areas of human interest.

3. Descartes attempted to perpetuate the centuries-old view that a human being is a composite of a physical part, the body, and a spiritual part, the soul (or mind). In the wake of generations of scientific research, this is an anachronism. Science today affirms that a human being is a highly developed biological organism, the product of eons of evolution and, contrary to what Descartes opines, thinking and willing occur in our brains, not a spiritual substance distinct from our bodies. Further, death takes place when the body shuts down, not when a soul departs. Gilbert Ryle (1900-1976), a twentieth-century British philosopher, gave us an alternative to Descartes' notion of a soul (or mind) as a spiritual substance distinct from the body. (10) "Mind," Ryle submits, is not a mysterious "Ghost in

a Machine," but a shorthand expression for brain-based behaviors which we exhibit routinely, such as texting a friend, driving a car, planning a vacation, researching a paper, diagnosing a health ailment, shopping, reading a book, doing a Google search, etc. Ryle says that Descartes made a "category mistake" by imagining that "mind" occupies a category distinct from these behaviors.

4. Next, Descartes claims to doubt *all* of his beliefs simultaneously. He waters this down a bit by observing that if he can show that the "foundation" of his beliefs is shaky, he must discard all of them. This type of doubt is suspect. When circumstances warrant, we can doubt one belief, or perhaps a handful, and the related practices, but that's it. When you discover that your friend Nicole has betrayed a confidence and spread malicious gossip about you, you reassess your belief that she is supportive and loyal, and you probably alter your practice of texting her several times a day. If you shop at a store which you believe is competitive, only to find that its prices on some items far exceed those at another store, you call that belief into question and you patronize the other store on a trial basis. If you believe a charity which you support does fine work but see a story in the news that nearly half of its income is spent on "administrative costs," you seek more information and question whether you should remain a donor. If you believe that a celebrity whom you admire is a responsible spouse and parent but learn via a highly publicized scandal that you've been mistaken all along, you reconsider quickly. This is typically what happens in our lives as reason to doubt a belief and a practice surfaces. It is far-fetched to say, as Descartes does, that we can doubt (and suspend) the entire gamut of our beliefs; indeed, I contend that it is psychologically impossible.

5. Finally, in the *Meditations*, Descartes reasons that his thinking (doubting) guarantees that he exists because he cannot think (doubt) unless he first exists as a being capable of thinking (doubting), that is, as a mind or soul. His Latin is "Cogito, ergo sum" – "I think, therefore I exist." But what exactly is this "I"? I submit that it cannot be what you or I mean by "I" or "me" or "self." Consider two widely held views about "self." One is that "self" is a product of one's links to people, places, things, and events in one's past which one retrieves with the aid of memory. On this view, self is a "social self" and your memory is the key to your personal identity

over time. The other is that "self" is linked to one's body; according to this view, certain features of your body (e.g., DNA) persist through the years so that your body is the key to your personal identity over time. Early in the *Meditations*, however, Descartes abandons physical reality due to its dependence on the senses, a flawed source. As a result, his "I," if indeed there is one, is a vague, nebulous entity distinct from his actual self.

The Tests of Truth

As we indicated above, just as statements are true, false, or meaningless, so too beliefs are true, false, or meaningless. (As we said earlier, true means accurate, correct, sound, justified, or reliable, and false means the opposite.) There are tests that we can use to help us decide which category a particular statement or belief falls into. Here we'll look at the three main classical tests of truth – coherence, correspondence, and pragmatic. As a rule of thumb, if a given statement tests true by all three tests, we have good reason to declare it true; on the other hand, if it tests false by all three, we have good reason to declare it false. Unfortunately, sometimes a statement lends itself to only one test, sometimes it tests positively on one test and negatively on another, and sometimes it isn't testable by any of the tests. In such cases, we face a predicament and the sensible position may be to say "I don't know" or "The statement is meaningless" or "The statement is faith-based."

The *coherence test of truth* reflects the fact that enculturation imbues in us hundreds of beliefs (and practices) which are popular in our culture or sub-culture. In many cases these beliefs have been proven beyond a reasonable doubt over the years (e.g., Smoking is hazardous to your health.). In other cases, they haven't been (e.g., There are angels.) but they remain popular nonetheless. (11) Given that there is a widely-accepted network of beliefs - conventional wisdom - and we wish to figure out whether a newly proposed claim is true, a simple and convenient way is to ask "Does it mesh with what we know (i.e., what is widely taken to be the case)?" If it does, we say it is true; if not, we say it is false. When we do this, we're applying the coherence test of truth. According to this test, *a claim is true if it is consistent with widely accepted beliefs and it is false if it isn't.* We use this test a lot in daily life, even if we're not aware that we do.

For instance, if a person says "Regular exercise promotes good mental and physical health," we accept this because it is consistent with widely accepted beliefs. We also use this test in specialized areas. For instance, if you go to your local pharmacist, George, to fill a prescription for warfarin, George will first access your records on the computer and then say: "I'm sorry but I can't fill this prescription. Warfarin and aspirin are both blood thinners and you're already on aspirin. Taking both is dangerous." Here your pharmacist defers to the conventional wisdom in his profession. (12)

The coherence test has clear advantages. It doesn't require us to do any heavy lifting. We don't have to gather facts or undertake experiments. And it usually serves us well. But it also has a downside. As history shows time and again, beliefs which are old and popular are not necessarily true. If you size up a belief based on its consistency with beliefs which later turn out to be false, your conclusion is likely flawed.

The *correspondence test of truth* can be described as the detective's test of truth. Suppose a wealthy woman, Jacquelyn Morris, is murdered around 9:00 p.m. on a Sunday in her mansion. As part of his investigation, Anthony Collier, the lead detective on the case, initially pinpoints a suspect but he finds no evidence linking her to the crime. After several weeks, though, he discovers that a security camera on the gate of an estate not far from Jacquelyn's property reveals that a van with the sign "Alex's Bakery" drove through the neighborhood the night of the murder. Collier then visits the bakery and summons the owner, Alex, to police headquarters for an interrogation. Initially, Alex reports that he was making a delivery. But pressed by Detective Collier, Alex can furnish neither the name nor the address of a customer in the area. Eventually Alex breaks down, confesses, and provides a full account of what took place. He reports that he and Sheilah murdered Jacquelyn because she had fired Sheilah as manager of a restaurant owned by Jacquelyn. They chose a Sunday for the crime, he admits, because they knew that Jacquelyn's domestic staff had Sundays off. In exchange for a prosecutor-approved reduced sentence, Alex testifies in court against Sheilah who gets life in prison. In this case Detective Collier sought out the facts relentlessly over weeks. Only when the facts clearly pointed to Alex and Sheilah did he charge them with the crime. This is the correspondence test in action. According to this test, *a claim is true if it is supported by the known relevant facts.*

The correspondence test works well when we have ready access to the facts and there is a consensus about the facts. Fortunately, that is often the case. This explains why we use this test so often. In some cases, however, we don't have ready access to the facts, or there's disagreement about the facts. Under these circumstances the correspondence test doesn't work as well as we'd like but that doesn't mean that we should abandon it. As in the investigation sketched above, the correspondence test may be the only test that holds out any hope for the discovery of truth. Just as only patient digging for facts by Detective Collier implicated Alex and Sheilah, so too, only patient digging for facts can reveal truth and falsity in a lot of other cases.

The final test is the *pragmatic test of truth*. The term pragmatic comes from the Greek word for *action* or *deed*, so this test requires us to undertake an action to figure out whether a statement is true or false. The pragmatic test, when it works well, is a conversation stopper. Two or more people often differ over a particular statement without settling on a strategy to determine who is right. The pragmatic test offers a strategy. For instance, suppose Janet and Alicia are talking about Sarah. Janet says "Sarah has an outstanding vocabulary" but Alicia doesn't buy it. They could go on arguing about it but one way to save time would be to invoke the pragmatic test. If they agree to do this, they will restate "Sarah has an outstanding vocabulary" in an *if..., then...* format. (Logicians call if-then sentences "conditionals." In conditionals the "if" clause is the *antecedent* and the "then" clause is the *consequent*.) The "if" clause would specify an action that they could take and the "then" clause would specify the results that will occur if "Sarah has an outstanding vocabulary" is true. Let's say they agree on this: "If we ask Sarah to work the Sunday *New York Times* crossword without a dictionary, then she will complete it with 100% accuracy in less than two hours." Or, "If we ask Sarah to define five terms - vicarious, homophobic, defenestration, goober, and largo, then she will give correct answers to at least four of them." So, according to the pragmatic test, *a claim is true, if, when you act upon it, you get predicted results*. To use this test effectively, the action in the *if* clause should be one that is *simple* and that *you control*, and the predicted *results* should be *easy to detect*. The more complex the action, the more you rely on others to take the action, and the more difficult it is to detect the results, the less likely the pragmatic test will work.

The pragmatic test often works well but it, too, runs into obstacles. There can be disagreement as to what action is appropriate in the "if" clause and what results should occur in the "then" clause. In the two examples above, for instance, Alicia may approve both as stated while Janet declines to do so. Janet might insist that in the first Sarah needs to complete the task in no more than one hour, and in the second Sarah should get ten terms to define and needs to get nine out of ten correct. These differences need to be worked out in all cases where more than one person has an interest. If Alicia and Janet cannot resolve their differences, one or both may turn out to be *radical skeptics*. (See below.) For the best results, the pragmatic test should be applied two or more times to a given claim.

All three tests have strengths and weaknesses. And all three have limits but this doesn't necessarily mean that the tests are flawed in principle. There may be no way to tell if some claims are true. Consider the following: "God loves you," "Mohammed is God's messenger," or "It was meant to be." None of the three tests holds much promise for any of these. Some who embrace claims such as these predict that we will learn that they are true when we die or when the world ends. This is called *eschatological verification*. Pascal's Wager (Chapter 2: Religion) falls into this category. Deferring a verdict on a disputed claim to a distant future (that may never occur) strikes me as an intellectual cop-out and a thinly disguised rationalization of dogma. What do you think?

Moderate and Radical Skepticism

To complete our discussion of knowledge, let's reflect briefly on the difference between *moderate skepticism* and *radical skepticism*. To be skeptical is to doubt. Since philosophy involves figuring out whether a particular belief is true or a particular practice is sensible and ethical, philosophy requires us to be skeptics. It requires us to doubt the belief and the practice, at least for a time. Those who hold that doubt usually leads to the discovery that the belief is or is not true and the practice is or is not sensible and ethical are moderate skeptics. Those who hold that doubt never leads to such a discovery, however, are radical skeptics. Radical skeptics, who are few and far between, hold that we cannot tell with confidence whether *any* claim is true or false. (13) They discount all tests of truth. They are basically agnostics, not just about God, but about all claims. They consider the quest for knowledge a fool's errand. In my view, radical skepticism is a flawed position which cannot be successfully defended for these reasons:

1. If a radical skeptic (RS) says "We can't know anything for sure," we can ask the RS whether he or she is sure about this claim. If the RS says, "yes," the RS contradicts the claim. If the RS says, "no," the RS withdraws the claim.
2. If the RS offers a defense of the claim, he or she assumes that the statements in the defense are true.
3. If you follow a RS through the day, you will find that he or she implicitly takes many claims to be true such as: "Eating food regularly is necessary to sustain life," "Bringing your car to a stop at a red light avoids accidents," and "Cell phones enable people at a distance to stay in touch with one another."

Footnotes:

1. I will use the terms statement and claim interchangeably in this chapter.

2. PASS explains why so many people believe in angels or a devil despite the fact that there is no proof of the existence of such entities. Remarkably, more people in the U.S. believe in angels (72%) and the devil (60%) than in evolution (45%), even though science has confirmed evolution overwhelmingly over the past century. See Michael Shermer, *The Believing Brain*, Times Books, p. 3.

3. Rene Descartes, *Meditations and Other Metaphysical Writings*, Translated with an Introduction by Desmond M. Clarke, Penguin Books, 2000, p. 18. All the quotations here are from the *Meditations*. The full title of this work provides insight into Descartes's intentions. It is *Meditations on First Philosophy in which The Existence of God and the Distinction of the Soul from the Body Are Demonstrated*. It was originally published in Latin in 1641.

4. *Ibid.*, p. 18.

5. *Ibid.*, pp. 18-19.

6. *Ibid.*, p. 19.

7. *Ibid.*, p. 63.

8. See Theodore Schick, Jr., and Lewis Vaughn, *How to Think About Weird Things*, Third Edition, McGraw-Hill, 2002, especially Chapter 3, "Looking for Truth in Personal Experience," and Terence Hines, *Pseudoscience and the Paranormal*, Prometheus Books, 2003, especially pages 21-32.

9. Two cognitive scientists confirm this. They write:

    > Reason is not disembodied, as the tradition has largely held, but arises from the nature of our brains, bodies, and bodily experiences... The same neural and cognitive mechanisms that allow us to perceive and move around also create our conceptual systems and modes of reason. To understand reason, we must understand the details of our visual system, our motor system, and the general mechanisms of neural binding. Reason is not a transcendent feature of the universe or of disembodied mind. Instead, it is shaped crucially by the peculiarities of our human bodies, by the remarkable details of the neural structure of our brains, and by the specifics of our everyday functioning in the world. George Lakoff and Mark Johnson, *Philosophy in the Flesh: The Embodied Mind and its Challenge to Western Thought*, Basic Books, 1999, p. 4.

10. See Gilbert Ryle, *The Concept of Mind*, University of Chicago Press, 1984; originally published in 1949. Ryle's position is reinforced by contemporary brain research as crystallized by a science journalist in the following paragraph:

    > The brain processes all the tasting, smelling, hearing, seeing and touching that we do throughout our lives. It regulates breathing and blood circulation. It stands guard

over us, ready to alert us to injuries and other problems through a messaging system called pain. And, of course, it's the place where all our thoughts and memories live. It is the beginning and end of us all. No brain, no you. Guy P. Harrison, *Think*, Prometheus Books, 2013, p. 55.

11. Supporters of the correspondence test of truth, which we'll discuss next, can argue that widely-accepted beliefs which have been proven beyond a reasonable doubt conform to *facts* which investigators have discovered, and for this reason the coherence test depends on the correspondence test. The correspondence test of truth is a fact-based test.

12. This is a case where you rely on your pharmacist as an expert and your pharmacist, in turn, relies on other experts.

13. One source of the radical skeptic's doubt about the reliability of claims is the gradual process of accumulating knowledge in an area. Typically, for instance, contemporary research will show that a prevalent belief, based on prior research, is mistaken in part or in whole. This can prompt the attitude that it is likely that future research will undercut beliefs based on current findings so that one needs to be wary of all claims. A related source of such doubt is a disagreement among recognized authorities in a field on an issue.

Recommendations for Further Study:

1. Terence Hines, *Pseudoscience and the Paranormal*, Prometheus Books, 1988.
2. Martin Gardner, *Science: Good, Bad, and Bogus*, Prometheus Books, 1981.
3. James Randi, *Flim Flam*, Prometheus Books, 1982.
4. Paul Kurtz, *In Defense of Secular Humanism*, Prometheus Books, 1983.
5. Paul Kurtz, *The New Skepticism: Inquiry and Reliable Knowledge*, Prometheus Books, 1992.
6. Michael Shermer, *Science Friction*, Times Books, 2005.
7. Michael Shermer, *The Believing Brain*, Times Books, 2011.
8. Israel Levine, *Francis Bacon*, Kennikat Press, 1970.
9. A. R. Skemp, *Francis Bacon*, Kennikat Press, 1970.
10. A. E. Taylor, *Thomas Hobbes*, Kennikat Press, 1970.
11. Morris Goran, *Fact, Fraud, and Fantasy*, A. S. Barnes and Co., Inc., 1979.
12. Richard Peters, *Hobbes*, Penguin Books, 1956.
13. John Dewey, *The Quest for Certainty*, Capricorn Books, 1960, originally published in 1929.
14. Brand Blanshard, *The Nature of Thought*, 2 Volumes, Allen & Unwin, 1939.
15. Bertrand Russell, *Philosophical Essays*, Simon & Schuster, 1966.
16. William James, *Pragmatism and the Meaning of Truth*, Harvard University Press, 1981.
17. Daniel C. Dennett, *Consciousness Explained*, Little, Brown, and Co., 1991; and *Darwin's Dangerous Idea*, Simon & Schuster, 1995.
18. Stephen Pinker, *How the Mind Works*, Norton, 1997.
19. John Searle, *Mind: A Brief Introduction*, Oxford University Press, 2004.
20. Sam Harris, *Free Will*, Free Press, 2012.
21. Eben Alexander, M.D., *Proof of Heaven: A Neurosurgeon's Journey into the Afterlife*, Simon & Schuster, 2012.
22. Sam Harris, *Waking Up: A Guide to Spirituality Without Religion*, Simon & Schuster, 2014.
23. Robert Burton, *A Skeptic's Guide to the Mind: What Neuroscience Can and Cannot tell Us About Ourselves*, Macmillan Publishers, 2013, and *On Being Certain: Believing You Are Right Even When You're Not*, St. Martin's Griffin, 2008.
24. Sally Satel and Scott Lilienfeld, *Brainwashed: The Seductive Appeal of Mindless Neuroscience*, Basic Books, 2013.
25. George Lakoff and Mark Johnson, *Philosophy in the Flesh: The Embodied Mind and its Challenge to Western Thought*, Basic Books, 1999.
26. Christopher Chabris and Daniel Simon, *The Invisible Gorilla: How Our Intuitions Deceive Us*, Crown, 2010.

27. Guy P. Harrison, *Think: Why You Should Question Everything*, Prometheus Books, 2013.

28. Daniel Kahneman, *Thinking Fast and Slow*, Farrar, Straus and Giroux, 2011.

29. Curtis White, *The Science Delusion: Asking the Big Questions in a Culture of Easy Answers*, Melville House, 2013.

Readings: Knowledge

Gilbert Ryle on Mind

Tom Shipka (2006)

The traditional view of mind in the West since the time of Plato, which was defended famously by Descartes in his *Meditations* of 1641, is that the mind is a non-physical and unobservable entity distinct from the body such that a human being is a composite of two substances, one incorporeal, the other corporeal, which interact mysteriously. This traditional view has been the target of growing skepticism in the modern era by many scientists and philosophers, including Gilbert Ryle.

Ryle was a twentieth-century British analytic philosopher who held that most traditional philosophical puzzles are really pseudo-problems due to misuses of language and confusion over concepts. In his 1949 *The Concept of Mind*, Ryle tried to point out the flaws in the traditional view of mind and body which he referred to derisively as "the dogma of the Ghost in the Machine." The main culprit, Ryle says, is language. When we use terms, we assume that they refer to entities. For instance, when we speak about a computer, car, or sofa, we take these terms as pointers to objects that we observe. Similarly, when we speak about a person as intelligent, witty, passionate, angry, or optimistic, we are tempted to see these terms as pointers to an object, a mind, that we do not observe. This is a mistake, Ryle insists, because mental terms refer not to a mysterious, hidden chamber but to a variety of observable human behaviors. Here Ryle reflects the post-Darwinian perspective that a human being is a highly developed biological organism with a complex and unique nervous system, the center of which is a remarkable three-pound organ called the brain, that enables humans to exhibit a wide variety of behaviors, many quite remarkable.

Ryle uses an analogy between a British university and a human being to show that the traditional view of mind is due to what he calls a "category mistake." Let's refer to a university that most of us are familiar with to see his point. If a visitor to Youngstown State University goes to Kilcawley Center, Maag Library, DeBartolo Hall, Stambaugh Stadium, classrooms, laboratories, the bookstore, and campus restaurants, and meets faculty, staff, students, and alumni attending a reunion, but then asks to see YSU, he or she wrongly assumes that what we call YSU is something distinct from the buildings, restaurants, learning sites, and people which taken together are YSU. Similarly, Ryle argues, a person who observes you send an e-mail, work a crossword puzzle, hang up on a telemarketer, tell a joke, or write a poem, but then asks to see your "mind," wrongly assumes that what we call your "mind" is something distinct from the observable, brain-based acts which you perform.

Has Ryle succeeded in dispatching the traditional view of mind and body to the trash heap of history? Hardly. Firstly, the traditional view is sustained by most religions and skeptics such as Ryle aren't even a blip on the radar screen of most religious people. Secondly, even if consciousness is brain-based, as neuroscientists say, they have not yet fully explained it on naturalistic grounds (and perhaps they never will). This gives aid and comfort to traditional dualists who treat the incompleteness in the scientific explanation of consciousness much like intelligent design advocates treat gaps in the fossil record supporting evolution. And thirdly, there is an ever-growing literature in the field of consciousness studies about near-death experiences and past-life memories that is fundamentally at odds with Ryle's viewpoint on several grounds. Thus, the merits of Ryle's critique aside, the traditional paradigm survives and prospers.

Eben Alexander's Journey into the Afterlife

Tom Shipka (2012)

There is a new convert to the belief that consciousness is not produced by or dependent on the brain. He is Eben Alexander, M.D., a distinguished neurosurgeon who spent much of his career on the Harvard medical faculty and who has authored 150 publications and delivered over 200 papers. (1) And what prompted this conversion? It was Dr. Alexander's near-death-experience in 2008 at age 54 while in a seven-day coma when he battled the rarest of illnesses – bacterial meningitis caused by *E. coli*. (2)

During his coma, the neo-cortex of Dr. Alexander's brain, which "is responsible for memory, language, emotion, visual and auditory awareness, and logic," shut down completely, he claims, making conscious experience impossible. Nevertheless, inexplicably, he began a spiritual journey that took him to three destinations. The first was a dark, Jello-O like, red-brown "muck," a mud pool with a rhythmic, pounding sound, that he calls "the Realm of the Earthworm's Eye." The second, which he calls the "Gateway," featured a bright light, captivating music and song, and an angel guide, a beautiful woman with high cheekbones, blue eyes, and golden-brown hair. Here, with his companion, he found himself in clouds flying over trees, fields, streams, waterfalls, and people. (3) The third, which he calls the "Core," was the culmination of his journey. In the Core, which he describes as "an orb-like ball of light," he encountered God, the all-powerful, all-loving, and all-knowing Creator, who gave him this message:

- God loves him and all others unconditionally;
- Evil is necessary on earth because without it human free will and human growth are impossible; (4) and
- Love will triumph over evil.

Remarkably, after his visit to the spiritual world, Dr. Alexander's "triple intravenous antibiotics" defeated the *E. coli* and, slowly but surely, he awoke from the coma, rediscovered his earthly self, which had been absent during his journey, and eventually resumed his professional practice. But he was now a changed person with an urgent mission: to share his journey with others - lay people, medical professionals, and scientists - to teach four lessons. They are that God loves all of us unconditionally, we are "spiritual beings currently inhabiting our evolutionarily developed mortal brains and bodies," we "get closer" to our genuine spiritual selves "by manifesting love and compassion" on earth, and the materialistic worldview embraced by many scientists is "mistaken." Scientists, he hoped, would learn, as he did on his journey, that: "The physical side of the universe is as a speck of dust compared to the invisible and spiritual part." (p. 82)

Although Dr. Alexander is convinced that his spiritual journey could not have been a hallucination (5), there are, as you would expect, plenty of skeptics, neurosurgeons among them. He invites skeptics near and far to do what he failed to do before his transformative journey, that is, to keep an open mind and to investigate the voluminous and ever-growing body of research on near-death and out-of-body experience. Only time will tell if skeptics will accept his invitation and, if they do, whether their doubts will fade.

1.   Eben Alexander, M.D., *Proof of Heaven: A Neurosurgeon's Journey into the Afterlife*, Simon & Schuster Paperbacks, 2012, p. 20. Future references to this book are by page number. A testimony to the importance of Alexander's reported experience comes from Raymond A. Moody, Jr., M.D., Ph.D., whose *Life After Life* in 1975 brought NDEs to public attention. Moody writes: "Dr. Eben Alexander's near-death experience is the most astounding I have heard in more than four decades of studying this phenomenon. (He) is living proof of an afterlife."

2.   When the antibiotics which Dr. Alexander received didn't seem to have an impact, his condition deteriorated to a point that his doctors saw only two possible outcomes – death or survival in a persistent vegetative state.

3.   Along the way, the angel guide, whom he calls "the Girl on the Butterfly Wing," revealed to him that he is loved unconditionally and that after his visit to the spiritual world, he would return to the earthly one.

4.   Philosophers will point out that there are at least two fundamental problems with this claim. The first is that it is not clear how an all-powerful God can bestow power on humans via free will and still remain all-powerful. The second is that, assuming free will exists, it helps to explain moral evil, that is, suffering caused by humans (e.g., murder, rape, burglary, identity theft, etc.) but not natural evil, that is, suffering caused by nature (e.g., hurricanes, tsunamis, tornadoes, etc.). The latter suffering remains God's doing and seems incompatible with the unconditional love which Alexander attributes to God.

5.   Alexander examines and dismisses a series of traditional neurological hypotheses to explain his experience while in a coma. See pp. 140-146 and Appendix B, pp. 185-188.

The Invisible Gorilla

Tom Shipka (2012)

In 1997 two psychologists designed an experiment in which they directed a group of volunteers to view a film that lasted less than a minute in which people assembled in a circle pass a basketball to one another. The viewers were asked to count the exact number of passes. Because they focused their attention on the movement of the ball, over half of them failed to notice something that they didn't expect. Midway through the film, a person dressed in a gorilla suit walked through the circle, stopped, faced the camera, beat its chest, and walked off, spending a full nine seconds in the film. The experiment has been repeated hundreds of times with the same results. (1)

Recently, the two psychologists, Christopher Chabris and Daniel Simons, published a book which expands on the gorilla experiment. Entitled *The Invisible Gorilla: How Our Intuitions Deceive Us*, (2) it demonstrates that all of us are victims of six illusions – attention, memory, confidence, knowledge, cause, and potential.

In the illusion of attention, highlighted in the gorilla experiment, we assume that we see far more of our visual field than we actually do. (3) In this connection, the authors urge people to discontinue the use of both hand-held and hands-free cell phones while driving because studies show that using a cell phone dramatically impairs our ability to perceive unexpected events. (4)

In the illusion of memory, we assume that we remember the past far more accurately than we actually do. (5) For instance, a former basketball player at Indiana University vividly remembered that Coach Bobby Knight had choked him in a rage of anger at a practice but a videotape of the event which surfaced later contradicted the player's story. (6)

In the illusion of confidence, we assume that self-assured people are competent people. (7) Studies show, however, that "the confidence that people project, whether they are diagnosing a patient, making decisions about foreign policy, or testifying in court" is no guarantee that they are as well-informed as they believe. (8)

In the illusion of knowledge, we assume that we know more about a topic than we usually do, whether we're talking about a bicycle, a toilet, a car, or a computer. If we're pressed for explanations, we usually come up short. (9)

In the illusion of cause, we mistake correlation with causality. (10) For instance, because many autistic children are first diagnosed soon after their vaccinations for measles, mumps, and rubella, many parents refuse to have their children vaccinated, despite the fact that dozens of studies with hundreds of thousands of children show that there is no causal link between autism and vaccinations. (11)

Finally, in the illusion of potential, we assume that "simple tricks can unleash the untapped potential" in our minds. (12) For instance, many parents play classical music to their babies to enhance their IQ, despite the fact that there is no scientific evidence to support such a belief. (13)

In a nutshell, then, Christopher Chabris and Daniel Simons challenge all of us to be on the lookout for the invisible gorillas, the everyday illusions that haunt us. To succeed, of course, we must first acknowledge that they exist.

1. This experiment demonstrates "inattention blindness," our tendency to miss unexpected objects in our surroundings because our attention is directed elsewhere. When this film was shown at a conference that I attended in Las Vegas in January 2005, most of the audience, myself included, missed the gorilla.

2. Broadway Paperbacks, 2009.

3. *The Invisible Gorilla*, p. 7.

4. *The Invisible Gorilla*, p. 25.

5. *The Invisible Gorilla*, p. 241.

6. *The Invisible Gorilla*, p. 73.

7. *The Invisible Gorilla*, p. 231.

8. *The Invisible Gorilla*, p. 82. In fact, the authors contend that "the most incompetent among us tend to be the most overconfident." (p. 95) An example of unjustified confidence that the authors use is George Tenet's answer to President George W. Bush's question as to whether Saddam Hussein really had weapons of mass destruction. Tenet replied: "It's a slam dunk." As it turned out, Tenet was wrong. (p. 95)

9. *The Invisible Gorilla*, pp. 121-123.

10. *The Invisible Gorilla*, pp. 231.

11. *The Invisible Gorilla*, pp. 174-176, p. 179. The authors note that "Despite the now-overwhelming evidence that vaccinations are not at all associated with autism, 29 percent of people in our national survey agreed with the statement 'vaccines given to children are partly responsible for causing autism.'" (p. 183)

12. *The Invisible Gorilla*, p. 242.

13. *The Invisible Gorilla*, pp. 185-197.

CHAPTER 4

Choices

An Overview

What is a Choice?

In this chapter we'll inquire whether our choices are *free*. Put differently, do we have *freedom* or *free will*? In Chapter 6, we'll revisit the terms *free* and *freedom* when we ask how much discretion a government should permit its citizens.

Let's say that your car needs four new tires. You visit three tire dealers and ask each to give you a bid on a specific make and size. One dealer's bid turns out to be much lower than the others, so you go with that one. You just made a choice. During a typical week, you make hundreds of them. Here is what happens when you make a choice:

- you encounter two or more possible courses of action at the same time,
- you identify each course,
- you reflect, at least briefly, on each course, and
- you select one course and reject the others.

These are the *elements* of a choice. Most of our choices are easy to make. They don't cause anxiety and we make them quickly. Some, however, are difficult to make. They do cause anxiety and we agonize over them. Choosing a space in a parking lot or a seat in a classroom or movie theater, for most of us, falls into the "easy" category; choosing whether to donate a kidney to a friend for an organ transplant or to accept an attractive job offer in a foreign country, for most of us, falls into the "difficult" category. The main question which has been asked for centuries about a choice is not whether it is easy or difficult - this can change from person to person - but "Is it free?"

A choice is free if it meets two criteria: **the person making the choice selects the course of action that he or she *wants*** and **the person making the choice *can select a different course* from the one that he or she actually selects**.

There are four basic theories about choices that we will study in this chapter – fatalism, predestination, determinism, and indeterminism - and three of them deny that any choices meet both criteria. To illustrate this, let's consider a trip that Ron is taking.

One Choice – Four Scenarios

Ron is driving alone two weeks before Christmas to visit his aunt and uncle who live over 500 miles away via interstates. He leaves early in the morning and plans to stop at the halfway point for lunch. As lunch time nears and he approaches an exit, he sees a "food" sign which lists Perkins, Cracker Barrel, McDonald's, and Arby's. He decides on Cracker Barrel where he orders coffee, biscuits and gravy, and the potato casserole. After lunch Ron gets back on the road but not until he buys gifts in the Cracker Barrel store for his aunt and uncle.

Here are four interpretations of Ron's choice of a site for lunch.

1. Fatalism: Ron was compelled to choose Cracker Barrel by a mysterious force called Fate that dictates all events in nature and history, including human choices. The script for his life, which he doesn't know and which he cannot change, has been written by Fate. Although it may have seemed to Ron that he could select one or more of the other restaurants, that feeling was illusory.

2. Predestination: Ron was compelled to choose Cracker Barrel by an all-powerful and all-knowing being - God - who dictates all events in nature and history, including human choices. The script for his life, which he doesn't know and which he cannot change, has been written by God. Although it may have seemed to Ron that he could select one or more of the other restaurants, that feeling was illusory.

3. Determinism: Ron was compelled to choose Cracker Barrel by his biological inheritance and his life experience. Given the DNA which his biological parents transmitted to him and the many influences which have

shaped him since his birth, he was necessitated to choose Cracker Barrel. Although it may have seemed to Ron that he could select one or more of the other restaurants, that feeling was illusory.

4. Indeterminism: Ron was *free* to choose Cracker Barrel and one or more of the other restaurants. At least two restaurants were compatible with his biological inheritance and his life experience. There were no causes – natural or supernatural – which compelled him to choose Cracker Barrel instead of another restaurant. When Ron made his choice, it seemed to him that he could select Cracker Barrel or one of the other restaurants and that he chose Cracker Barrel because he wanted to and not because he was compelled to.

Let's discuss each of these interpretations of choices.

The Basic Positions

Fatalism

Fatalism is the theory that a powerful and mysterious force called Fate dictates all events in nature and history, including all human choices. It affirms that when Ron chose Cracker Barrel, he was conforming to the plan of his life that Fatalism had scripted for him from time immemorial. Fatalism has adherents in popular culture but none, to my knowledge, among philosophers. The reason is that fatalism is a faith-based belief and fatalists simply state their belief without attempting to provide any proof for it. (One wonders what such a proof would look like.) Fatalism is reflected in sayings such as "It was meant to be," "It was her fate," "It was his destiny," "It was inevitable," "*Que sera, sera* (What will be, will be)," "He died because his number was up," and "Everything happens for a reason."

Years ago a student informed me that he was a fatalist. I asked him if he planned to study for our test next week. He said, "Why do you ask?" I replied, "As a fatalist, you believe that your grade is a done deal. You cannot alter it. So why waste time studying?" His reply? "If I study, I was fated to study; if I don't, I wasn't." He ducked my question and simply reaffirmed his belief as though it were a revelation from on high. He gave no way to confirm or disconfirm it. For him, merely articulating his position in a bold, confident voice was enough.

He is not alone. I have heard similar sentiments over the years by celebrities on TV talk shows. The host says "I understand that you're a fatalist. I'm not sure I get that. What exactly does it mean?" The guest replies:

I believe that there's something behind the way things happen that is just eerie. Let me give you an example. I just got my first role in a Broadway musical. I'd like to pat myself on the back for that but I can't. So many things beyond my control came together in just the right way at just the right time for me to get it. The actor who had been offered the role turned it down in a dispute over salary. A musician in the orchestra whom I happened to see at a delicatessen tipped me off that the role was up for grabs again. The original director, who had turned me down once before for summer stock, dropped dead in the theater. The new director was willing to stick his neck out to pick a newcomer over three Broadway veterans. And on the day of my audition, I was really on, despite the fact that I had a cold and a headache. It was my best audition ever. You see, there was such an amazing convergence of things. So many things that had to fall into place did. I didn't make it all happen. And it's too far-fetched to be dumb luck or happy coincidence. There's more to it than that. I think it was fate.

Usually the host smiles and says "I see. How fascinating. I've felt exactly the same way at times in my own life." What the host should have said is:

- "Is there any way that we can prove that fatalism is true? If so, how?"
- "I get the impression that fatalism reduces us to puppets on a string. Are you saying that we're powerless to shape our lives and that the future is out of our control?"
- "This sounds a lot like predestination. Do you think that God is the power behind the scenes orchestrating all this? If not, what is?"

Alas, the host says none of this. Unfortunately, entertainment usually trumps critical thinking.

The fact is that fatalism is a dogma. (On dogma, see Chapter 1: Introduction). It is also inimical to personal initiative and personal responsibility. If you truly believe that the future is settled and beyond your control, why would you exert energy to achieve goals? Why would you plan? Why would you hold yourself accountable for your actions? Why would you hold others accountable for their actions? Fatalism encourages passive acceptance, laziness, and rationalization.

Predestination

Predestination is a theory which affirms that the direct and immediate cause of all events, including human choices, is a spiritual and eternal being, God, whose power, knowledge, and goodness have no limits. Predestination claims that "God has a plan for each of us." When Ron chose Cracker Barrel, he was conforming to God's plan for him - God's script - whether he realized it or not. A lot of common statements are laced with predestination: "If you want to make God laugh, tell him **your** plans," "The entire family survived the fire, thanks be to God," and "You'll be back on your feet in no time, God willing." According to predestination, our dependence on God is complete. We cannot even take a breath unless God wills it. If God were to stop thinking of a blade of grass, or a bug, or a gorilla, or a human being, or a galaxy, even for a millisecond, *poof!* - It's gone instantly. Further, God "elects" those who will enjoy everlasting happiness in heaven as well as those who will suffer everlasting torment in hell. What a job description!

Jonathan Edwards (1703-1758), a philosopher-theologian from the American colonial period, who supported predestination, admits that this doctrine of the *elect* came to him with difficulty when he was young but, as he matured, he warmed up to it. He writes:

> From my childhood up, my mind has been full of objections against the doctrine of God's sovereignty, in choosing whom he would to eternal life, and rejecting whom he pleased; leaving them eternally to perish, and be everlastingly tormented in hell. It used to appear as a horrible doctrine to me. But I remember the time very well, when I seemed to be convinced, and fully satisfied, as to this sovereignty of God, and his justice in thus eternally disposing of men, according to his sovereign pleasure. (1)

Most Christians in the past two centuries have not followed Edwards's lead. Instead, ala John Hick - see *God and Suffering* in Chapter 2 - they affirm that God bestowed free will upon humans, empowering us to direct the course of our lives, to choose good or evil, and to merit salvation. (To predestination, this is heresy for it compromises the sovereignty of God according to which God is the sole and exclusive power in existence.) If we follow Edwards, however, Hick's arguments become irrelevant. With Edwards we repudiate human freedom and autonomy. We see humans as mere instruments in God's "hands." We chalk up everything - good *and evil* - to God. This is too much to swallow for most Christians. There is much on the good side of the ledger but there is also much on the evil side of the ledger. Over 12,000 diseases are God's doing. Hurricanes, tornadoes, tsunamis, and earthquakes are God's doing. War, murder, rape, fraud, arson, racism, sexism, and terrorism are God's doing. Doesn't this make God a moral monster? Who would wish to worship such a being?

Aside from all this, let us remember that predestination, like fatalism, is a faith-based doctrine. The foundation of predestination – *There is an all-powerful, all-knowing, and all-good God who is the direct and immediate cause of all events in nature and history* – is a mere assertion without proof.

Before we leave the topic of predestination, let me spring a surprise on you. You might think that the words "free" and "freedom" have no place in predestination literature. Wrong. According to Jonathan Edwards, you and I conform to God's plan every second of every day. Nevertheless, our choices are "free," he insists, *if we do what we want to do (despite the fact that God determines what we want to do)*. He writes:

> The plain and obvious meaning of the words *Freedom* and *Liberty*, in common speech, is *power, opportunity, or advantage, that any one has, to do as he pleases.* Or, in other words, his being free from hinderance (sic) or impediment in the way of doing, or conducting in any respect, as he wills. And the contrary to Liberty, whatever name we call that by, is a person's being hindered or unable to conduct as he will, or being necessitated to do otherwise. (2)

Example. You want a Big Mac for lunch, so you go to McDonald's, order one, and eat it. God caused you to want a Big Mac, God caused you to go to McDonald's, God caused you to order it, and God caused you to eat it. Nevertheless, your choice is free because *you got what you wanted*! Thus, Edwards and other predestinationists recognize only one criterion for a free choice: the person makes a free choice if he or she selects the course of action that he or she wants. We'll see a similar stance below in a secular theory called *soft-determinism*.

Determinism – Hard and Soft

Determinism is the theory that all our choices are caused by our biological inheritance and our life experience since we were born. As this applies to our story about Ron, a determinist holds that Ron's past compelled him to go to Cracker Barrel such that he could not possibly have chosen a different restaurant, even though he may have felt that he could. Determinists apply the principle of causality – all events have causes – to human choices. Although they do not claim that they can show a direct cause and effect link between a person's choice and his or her past in all cases, they argue that 1) it makes sense to apply the principle of causality to choices, and 2) as we gain more knowledge about human behavior over the years, as we're doing steadily, we'll eventually be able to show such a link. So, what explanation would a determinist give about Ron's choice of Cracker Barrel? It might go this way:

- Ron's parents are generous people and their habits have rubbed off on Ron. Ron, who wants to buy gifts for his aunt and uncle, is drawn to Cracker Barrel because his aunt and uncle love country music and Cracker Barrel has a huge variety of country CDs.
- Ron's all-time favorite breakfast, which was a staple in his house as he grew up in Georgia, is biscuits and gravy, a popular Cracker Barrel feature.
- Ron, who is chronically cold due to hypothyroidism, which runs in his family, knows that he will be warm if he gets a table near the fireplace at Cracker Barrel.
- Recently, at the urging of his stock broker, Ron bought 400 shares of Cracker Barrel, and he wants to help the chain to succeed so that his investment pays off.

According to determinists, when we choose a course of action (Cracker Barrel instead of Perkins, Arby's, or McDonald's), we choose the course that we choose by necessity. There's no wiggle room, given our biological and sociological past. This rules out any possibility for a choice to be free. Why? Because a choice is free if and only if the chooser selects the course of action which he or she wants and the chooser can select any of two or more possible courses of action. Alas, since the second criterion is never met, there are no free choices!

Or are there? Suppose a determinist takes a position similar to Jonathan Edwards. (See predestination above.) He or she would then argue that a choice is *free* if the course that you choose is the course that you *want* to choose, whether or not you can choose a different one. Back to Ron. Although he was compelled to choose Cracker Barrel due to his biological inheritance and his life experience, his choice is free because he wanted to go to Cracker Barrel.

Determinists who tell us that Ron's choice was not free because it was compelled by his biological and sociological past are called *hard determinists* and determinists who tell us that Ron's choice, although compelled by causes from his past, was nevertheless free because he did what he wanted to do, are called *soft determinists*. Further, since soft determinists hold that Ron's choice was *both determined (necessitated by his past)* **and** *free (he did want he wanted to do)*, they are also called *compatibilists*. Compatibilism affirms that there is no contradiction in saying that the same choice is both determined and free. (3)

Indeterminism

Indeterminism, also called *libertarianism* from *liber*, the Latin word for free, is the theory that some - not all - choices are free because the chooser selects the course that he or she wants to choose, and the chooser can select a course different from the one he or she actually chooses. Advocates of this position say that determinists make a mistake when they assume that nature and nurture compel a person to choose the specific course of action that he or she chooses in all cases. The past is compatible with multiple possible courses in many cases, they insist. Let's return to Ron's choice of biscuits and gravy. Even if we concede the point about Ron's special attraction to this dish, suppose the restaurant has run out of it. Now Ron must pick another item from the menu. Many of us have been in similar predicaments. Our favorite dish is gone; now we have to pick another. Ron looks at the menu and finds several items that he likes. If he finally opts for pecan pancakes, are we to conclude that this was necessitated? If we ask Ron whether he felt that he had the power to choose dishes other than pecan pancakes, I would be amazed if he said "no."

Thus, the case for indeterminism rests mainly on an argument from personal experience. When I make choices, I often seem to have the power to select any of several possible courses of action which I identify. For instance, when I look over a menu in a restaurant, I feel that I have the power to select several of the entrees listed. If I order lasagna, I am confident that I could have chosen steak, chicken, tortellini, pork chops, fish, or another dish instead. So, the choice of lasagna strikes me as free – I have selected what I want and I could have selected differently. Now, if determinism is correct, my experience is an illusion; the determinist insists that given my past, I was compelled to choose lasagna and I could not possibly have chosen a different entrée. Can the determinist prove this? Can he or she prove that causes in my past – my biological inheritance and my life experience – dictated lasagna and only lasagna? I don't think so. Absent such proof, the belief confirmed when we make choices, namely, that our past is compatible with multiple possibilities in the present, is justified. Test yourself. When you make a choice – say you choose an assortment of clothes to wear or a radio station to listen to or a friend to text - don't you seem to have the power to choose any of two or more possibilities?

The Range of Freedom

There's another aspect of choices that we need to consider. Determinists draw attention to influences from our past when we make choices. Although I object to their blanket claim that my past dictates the course that I choose in a lockstep fashion, I share their sensitivity to our backgrounds. Let's introduce the notion of the *range of freedom* which encompasses two dimensions - the *range of choices* and the *range of possibilities*. Your background – biological and sociological – weighs heavily on the array of choices that you face and the richness of the possibilities that you face. Take two hypothetical people - Sharon and Ricky. Sharon is an only child. Her father is a cardiologist and her mother is an architect. Their joint income exceeds $700,000 a year and they have a stable, successful marriage. Ricky lives with his grandparents because his mother died from a drug overdose. He doesn't know his father. His grandfather collects disability and his grandmother works part-time in a convenience store. The grandparents' income is less than $30,000 a year. Consider the choices that Sharon and Ricky face as they grow up. When it comes to health care, clothes, cars, electronic devices, furniture, vacations, hobbies, computers, education, employment, restaurants, food, entertainment, and much more, Sharon will very likely face more choices than Ricky and Sharon will very likely face more possibilities in these choices than Ricky. Sharon has both a *greater range of choices* and a *greater range of possibilities* in those choices. This is a fact of life. Based on this, we can speak justifiably about some individuals as *freer* than others.

Impediments and Coercion

In this discussion of whether choices are free, for the sake of simplicity, I have assumed that a chooser can act upon her choice without impediment. An impediment is an obstacle, a hindrance, which prevents a chooser from acting on a choice which she has made. If there is such an impediment, it changes the ball game. For instance, imagine that as Ron nears the strip of restaurants, he finds that all except McDonald's are closed because an accident has snapped the nearby power lines. Suddenly, Ron faces only one possible course of action - McDonald's - and he can no longer do what he wants to do, i.e., go to Cracker Barrel. Indeterminists and soft determinists would agree that under the circumstances his choice - if indeed there is one here - is not free.

A related issue is coercion. Coercion can change the circumstances sufficiently to destroy the freedom of the choice. This can apply in two cases – when you are forced to do something that you want to do and when you are forced to do something that you don't want to do. For instance, say you choose to visit a branch bank to inquire about a mysterious charge to your checking account. You choose to visit the bank first and to defer other chores – stopping at the gas station, texting a friend, going to the car wash, picking up a prescription – until later, and you want to visit the bank. As you leave your car, a stranger grabs your arm and says, "I have a gun. Do what I say. Walk into the bank in front of me to one of the tellers." The stranger plans to rob the bank and to use you as a hostage. On the one hand, you are forced to do something that you want to do – visit the bank. On the other hand, you are forced to do something that you don't want to do – serve as a hostage. Again, indeterminists and soft-determinists would likely agree that, under the circumstances, your choice to visit the branch is not free.

Responsibility and Punishment

Two related issues which lurk beneath the surface of the debate over choices are responsibility and punishment. Should we hold a person responsible - accountable - for his or her choices and, especially when a choice harms others, should we punish - inflict pain and suffering - on that person. According to hard and soft determinists, since you are compelled to do what you do and you couldn't possibly have done differently, responsibility and punishment are suspect. According to indeterminists, on the other hand, if your choice is free - you choose a course of action without compulsion – responsibility and punishment are justified. But this needs some fine tuning. The major theories of punishment are retribution, rehabilitation, deterrence, and incapacitation.

- *Retribution* involves punishing a wrongdoer because he or she freely injured others and therefore deserves to suffer. Support for this comes mainly from indeterminists but not from determinists.
- *Rehabilitation* involves reconditioning or reeducating wrongdoers to alter their habits. Support for this comes from both indeterminists and determinists. Determinists, however, do not consider this punishment.
- *Deterrence* involves punishing wrongdoers to dissuade them from a repetition of crime in the future, usually by appealing to their self-interest. (*"It's not in your self-interest to do things which will likely cause you to suffer again!"*) Support for deterrence comes from both indeterminists and determinists but, as in rehabilitation, determinists do not consider it punishment.
- *Incapacitation* involves removing a habitual wrongdoer from society to protect innocent citizens. Incapacitation can involve the death penalty or confinement for life or confinement for an extended period. The targets of incapacitation are typically habitual wrongdoers, such as serial murderers or rapists, especially those who fail to respond to rehabilitation and deterrence; a person who commits a single despicable act, such as assassination of a president, mass murder, or a terrorist attack; and mentally ill people who are prone to violence. In principle, both determinists and indeterminists can support incapacitation but, once again, determinists do not consider it punishment.

American philosopher, Sidney Hook, presented an argument justifying punishment as a deterrent to future misbehavior. His argument, he felt, makes sense whether choices are free or not. It can be formulated this way:

Society needs rules and laws to maintain order, protect rights, and promote happiness.

People who violate these rules and laws need to be punished to discourage such violations in the future.

Therefore, punishment of wrongdoers is justified. (4)

The argument makes an important assumption - people are dissuaded from crime by the threat of pain and suffering. Do you believe that this assumption is warranted? I believe that it is but only if we acknowledge that there are exceptions: deterrence simply doesn't work for everyone. Some people who are intent on a crime, for one reason or another, don't worry about what may follow it, even death.

Footnotes:

1. Jonathan Edwards, *Freedom of the Will*, in Muelder, Sears, and Schlabach, *The Development of American Philosophy*, Second Edition, Houghton Mifflin Company, 1960, p. 38.

2. Jonathan Edwards in Herbert W. Schneider, *A History of American Philosophy*, Second Edition, Columbia University Press, 1963, pp. 13-14.

3. Here's another example of a soft-determinist interpretation of a choice. Say that Zachary grew up on a family farm where he learned a farmer's skills, found the work exhilarating, and made dozens of friends among farm families. Later Zachary goes to college and chooses a major in agronomy. Although no one who knew him was surprised by his choice of major - many friends and relatives had predicted it for years - the choice was free because Zachary wanted to major in agronomy.

4. Sidney Hook, *The Quest for Being*, Prometheus Books, 1991. See especially "Moral Freedom in a Determined World."

Recommendations for Further Study:

1. Gary Gutting, *What Makes Free Will Free*, New York Times, October 19, 2011.
2. *John Martin Fischer, Robert Kane, Derk Pereboom, and Manuel Vargas, Four Views on Free Will, Blackwell Publishing, 2007.*
2. Clarence Darrow, *Crime, Its Causes and Treatment*, Forgotten Books, 2007.
3. *Attorney for the Damned: Clarence Darrow in the Courtroom*, Edited by Arthur Weinberg, University of Chicago Press, 1989.
4. Irving Stone, *Clarence Darrow for the Defense*, New American Library, 1969.
5. Clarence Darrow, *The Story of My Life*, Da Capo Press, 1996, especially Chapter 27.
6. Sidney Hook, *The Hero in History*, Beacon Press, 1955.
7. Sidney Hook, *The Quest for Being*, Prometheus Books, 1991.
8. Sidney Hook, *Determinism and Freedom in the Age of Modern Science*, New York University Press, 1958.
9. John Watkins, *Human Freedom After Darwin*, Open Court, 1999.
10. William James, *The Dilemma of Determinism*, Unitarian Review, 1884. Reprinted many times.
11. Jean-Paul Sartre, *Existentialism*, translated by Bernard Frechtman, Philosophical Library, 1947.
12. Bruce N. Waller, *Chanelle, Sabrina, and the Oboe*, in Shipka and Minton, *Philosophy: Paradox and Discovery*, Fifth Edition, McGraw-Hill, 2004.
13. *Great Crimes of the Century*, Blockbuster Entertainment, 1998.
14. Sam Harris, *Free Will*, Free Press, 2012.
15. Helen Steward, *A Metaphysics for Freedom*, Oxford University Press, 2012.
16. David Hodgson, *Rationality + Consciousness = Free Will*, Oxford University Press, 2012.
17. Robert Burton, *A Skeptic's Guide to the Mind: What Neuroscience Can and Cannot Tell Us About Ourselves*, Macmillan Publishers, 2013.
18. Sally Satel and Scott Lilienfeld, *Brainwashed: The Seductive Appeal of Mindless Neuroscience*, Basic Books, 2013.
19. Edward O. Wilson, *The Meaning of Human Existence*, Liveright, 2014, especially Chapter 14, Free Will, pp. 159-170.
20. Daniel C. Dennett, *Intuition Pumps and Other Tools for Thinking*, W. W. Norton & Co., 2013.
21. Alfred R. Mele, *Free: Why Science Hasn't Disproved Free Will*, Oxford University Press, 2014.
22. John Lemos, *Freedom, Responsibility, and Determinism: A Philosophical Dialogue*, Hackett Publishing Company, Inc., 2013.
23. Bruce N. Waller, *The Stubborn System of Moral Responsibility*, The MIT Press, 2014.
24. Rafael Yuste and George M. Church, "The New Century of the Brain," *Scientific American*, March 2014, pp. 38-45.

Readings: Choices

Free Will on Trial

Tom Shipka (2012)

As I collapse into my recliner to watch a network newscast, I recall the ones available, and then, without coercion, I consciously select the one I want. In other words, my choice is free. Or is it? Let's see if an experiment will tell us.

Suppose that Sue, a scientist, instructs me to look at pictures on a screen and to press a button with my right or left hand within five seconds after a sailboat appears. Suppose, further, that while I'm doing this, Sue uses a neuroimaging device to track the activity in the prefrontal cortex of my brain. After the sailboat appears a dozen times, Sue shows me that brain waves in the two hemispheres revealed which button I would press **before** I consciously chose to do so.

In fact, variations of this experiment have been performed hundreds of times by dozens of researchers with similar results. (1) And what does this research tell us?

According to many scientists, it tells us that free will is an illusion. Among them is Sam Harris, a neuroscientist. Harris writes:

> Some moments before you are aware of what you will do next – a time in which you subjectively appear to have complete freedom to behave however you please – your brain has already determined what you will do. You then become conscious of this 'decision' and believe that you are in the process of making it. (2)

Thus, for Harris, my choice to watch the news on NBC last night was triggered by unconscious events in my brain beyond my control. Indeed, all our choices, he insists, are the product of "background causes of which we are unaware and over which we exert no conscious control." (3)

What are we to make of this? Here are three points that we should consider.

- Firstly, the research done so far deals with simple choices covering a few seconds. Many of our choices, however, are complex and drawn-out. They often involve careful reflection on options, evaluation of likely results, and sometimes confusion, stress, and reassessment. The research on simple choices may not apply to complex ones.

- Secondly, as philosopher Alfred Mele argues, even if an action begins before we are conscious of it, our conscious self may still retain the power to "approve, modify, or ... cancel ... the action." (4) In this connection, all of us can probably recall instances when we suppressed urges toward anger or violence.

- Thirdly, whether choices are free or not, people need to be held accountable. If behavior reflects nature and nurture, as science tells us, then we must structure an environment which promotes civility. This means three things: punishment of wrongdoers to deter them and others from crime; rehabilitation of those wrongdoers for whom there is hope; and long-term imprisonment, or perhaps death, for those hardened criminals for whom there is no hope. A serial murderer must be stopped whether he acts freely or compulsively. (5)

Finally, if the sharp exchanges about these issues in the scientific and philosophical literature today are a clue, there is no end in sight to the centuries-old debate over free will versus determinism.

1. Benjamin Libet pioneered this research in the 1980s. For information about Libet and subsequent research, see Sam Harris, *Free Will*, Free Press, 2012, pp. 8-9, and pp. 69-76, and the "Neuroscience of Free Will," *Wikipedia*, pp. 1-15.

2. Harris, p. 9.

3. Harris, p. 5.

4. *Wikipedia*, p. 8. The power of the conscious self to veto an unconscious impulse or urge is sometimes called "free won't." Libet, arguably the first to link conscious choices with unconscious causes experimentally, claimed that the conscious self retains this power. Sam Harris, however, challenges it. (After this commentary aired, Michael Shermer, who writes the *Skeptic* column in *Scientific American*, critiqued Sam Harris's position. See Michael Shermer, "Free Won't," *Scientific American*, August 2012, p. 86.)

5. Harris, a determinist, concedes the need for deterrence, rehabilitation, and, to some extent, retribution. See pp. 56 et ff.

Leopold and Loeb

Tom Shipka (2005)

Clarence Darrow, a world famous defense attorney who grew up in Trumbull County, Ohio, took a case late in his career in Chicago in 1924 involving Nathan Leopold, Jr., and Richard Loeb, two brilliant Chicago teen-agers from wealthy families. Leopold and Loeb were fascinated with philosopher Friedrich Nietzsche's doctrine of the *ubermensch*, or "superman," a self-directed and defiant person who spurns the values, customs and laws of the herd. They decided to demonstrate their superiority by committing a perfect crime.

But it wasn't so perfect, after all. Within days after they kidnapped and murdered fourteen-year-old Bobby Franks, they were arrested by Chicago detectives and they confessed. The case against them was so formidable that Darrow abandoned any hope of acquittal, pleaded them guilty at the start of the trial, and fought to save their lives.

Clarence Darrow brought his deeply held philosophical belief in determinism, hard determinism specifically, to the courtroom. Hard determinism is the view that nature and nurture shape individuals to think and act as they do. To the hard determinist, the individual is neither free nor responsible. The saint deserves no applause; the sinner deserves no blame. Neither could possibly avoid doing what they had done given their past.

This was the first time in his career that Darrow applied determinism to the elite because he was accustomed to representing political radicals and the underprivileged. He said in his summation:

> ...*Your Honor, it is just as often a great misfortune to be the child of the rich as it is to be the child of the poor. Wealth has its misfortunes. Too much, too great opportunity and advantage, given to a child has its misfortunes...*

To the shock and amazement of virtually everyone, the judge sentenced the boys to life in prison instead of death. People shouldn't have been so surprised. During his career Darrow represented over 100 clients accused of murder and not one got the death penalty. Richard Loeb was murdered in prison and Nathan Leopold eventually won parole.

Today we continue to agonize over the issues at the heart of the Leopold-Loeb case - personal responsibility and punishment of wrongdoers. Are criminals helpless pawns of nature and nurture, compelled by causes in their past beyond their control to commit crimes, as Darrow argued? If so, punishment, particularly the death penalty, is suspect. Or, on the other hand, are criminals free agents who have the power to obey or disobey the law? If so, punishment, perhaps including the death penalty, is a mandate of justice.

Long after the Leopold-Loeb trial, American Pragmatist philosopher Sidney Hook challenged Darrow's position on punishment. Conceding for the sake of argument that hard determinism is true, Hook reasoned that civilization requires rules, and that punishment of those who violate such rules is indispensable to ensure compliance with them. Hook expected that the effective threat of punishment will deter rationally self-interested persons from crime because they believe that their loss is likely to outstrip their gain. This was Hook's justification for punishment in a determined world.

Everything Happens for a Reason (or It Was or Wasn't Meant to Be)

Tom Shipka (2005)

Occasionally, I hear the sayings "Everything happens for a reason," "It was meant to be," and "It wasn't meant to be," in my philosophy classes, in casual conversations, or in televised interviews.* When a speaker drops one of these lines in a conversation, it's as though something (a) very profound and (b) obviously true has been proclaimed. Unfortunately, the speaker usually gives no follow-up clarification of what he or she takes this pronouncement to mean, much less any explanation of why it is true. What, then, does "Everything happens for a reason" or "It was or wasn't meant to be" really mean, and is it true?

If you have an opportunity to interrogate people who make these statements about what they mean, you will find that it means different things to different people and sometimes different things to the same person. Here are some of the more popular interpretations of this saying:

1. *Natural events in the present follow from natural events in the past.* This version is expressed in comments such as "Alexis failed her history exam because she didn't study" or "Ralph has lung cancer due to thirty years of smoking." Had Alexis studied or Ralph abstained from tobacco, the implication is that Alexis would be celebrating her success or Ralph's lungs would be clear.

2. *All events happen by necessity according to a grand plan such that these events could not possibly unfold any differently.* Some attribute this grand plan to a deity as in the statement: "George died yesterday because he had finished all the work on earth that God had assigned to him." This view is theistic determinism which is also called predestination. Others attribute the grand plan to a non-deistic and inscrutable cosmic force, as in the statement: "George died yesterday because his number was up." This, of course, is fatalism. The implication is that if God or fate had scripted things differently, George would be chugging beer with the boys as he usually does at this hour of the day on his way home from work.

3. *All events, even unfortunate or tragic ones, have a beneficial result that explains or justifies these events.* This version is found in statements such as "Stephanie has stopped drinking since her DUI" or "The South Asian tsunami brought together a divided world in sympathy and compassion for the victims" or "The spread of Ebola to two nurses in Texas has prompted new safeguards for health care workers across the nation." The implication is that evil is inevitable, but that evil spawns good.

4. *The actual causes of many events are not the apparent causes but surprising and inconspicuous ones.* Thus, a person prone to conspiracy theory might allege that "FDR knew about the Japanese plan to attack Pearl Harbor in 1941, but he chose not to expose it because he wanted the attack to draw America into the war." The implication is that things are not what they seem; dark and dirty secrets lie behind events in the news.

5. *The events which occur in a person's life are determined by the moral quality of his or her previous life.* A Hindu or Buddhist who believes in karma might observe: "Fred must have done awful things in his last incarnation to suffer so many painful afflictions the past few years." The implication is that a cosmic justice is at work such that those deserving success or failure, happiness or sorrow, reward or punishment, eventually receive their due.

6. *The cause of some natural events is non-natural - God.* This view is expressed in statements such as "AIDS is God's way to punish homosexuals" or "Amy's recovery shows that God answered our prayers." The implications are that there is a transcendent entity that influences or controls the natural realm and that there are ways, such as prayer, for humans to solicit or produce interventions by this entity.

Are any of these versions of "Everything happens for a reason" or "It was or wasn't meant to be" true? Can any be adequately justified by arguments and facts?

Version 1 (previous events in nature cause present events in nature) has strong support in ordinary experience and scientific investigation. The causes of some events are difficult to pin down, however, and the implications of this version for human conduct are a subject of great controversy and continuing debate among philosophers and scientists. Are the causes at work in our lives compatible with the freedom that so many of us believe that we have?

Next, it seems clear that three versions cannot be proven and that they rest solely on faith. These include the fatalist rendition of version 2 (grand plan), version 5 (karma), and version 6 (God intervenes in nature at times). Version 6 also seems to require one to set aside Ockham's Razor, which suggests that we should always seek the simplest adequate solution or explanation. If a simpler explanation of an event seems quite adequate, why should we pass it by for a more complex one? (If Phoebe recovers from a severe cold after she receives an antibiotic, must we explore further?) Also, version 6 must deal with the apparent failure of the great majority of petitionary prayers and the selective nature of God's largesse. Why does God grant the prayers of the Smiths but not the Joneses, the Allens, the Stewarts, etc.? Why do some patients leave the hospital on foot and others in a hearse?

Next, the predestination rendition of version 2 (grand plan) requires one to prove the existence of a God that is the direct and immediate cause of all events. Even if success here is possible, which is doubtful if we recall the flurry of criticisms of each of the standard arguments for the existence of God, the fallout is considerable. Human free will is ruled out by such a God, and both good and evil are God's doing. If we take this path, must we next deny the reality of evil to salvage God's reputation?

Version 3 (happy endings) runs into two problems. First, some events seem to trigger few if any beneficial or desirable side effects. Consider the beloved young child whose death drives the mother first to depression and later to suicide or the crack addict who abandons his wife and children, wrecks his career, and turns to crime to support his habit until he takes his own life out of despair and disgust. Not all endings are happy ones. Second, while it is often possible to find a benefit in even the worst calamities, it is seldom the case that the benefit explains or justifies the calamity on a cost-benefit analysis. An earthquake destroys a school and kills half or more of the students. This triggers a boon for local funeral directors after a protracted period of relatively few deaths, and an erection of an impressive new school with state-of-the-art technology and smaller classes. Does it make sense to say that these "benefits" justify the deaths of the children? Would one be willing, if one could, to replicate such calamities across the planet for the sake of their beneficial effects in all societies? Only the most morally depraved and cold-hearted among us could possibly answer in the affirmative.

Version 4 (many causes are hidden) has the merit of urging thoroughness and caution in the search for truth. Our explanations of events are sometimes mistaken, as the conviction and imprisonment of innocent persons attest. But version 4 also has liabilities. It can invite excessive skepticism and stubbornness, causing one to look needlessly beyond adequate explanations. When the facts clearly support a hypothesis or conclusion, reasonable people should acknowledge it and move on. Facts should trump biases, hopes, wants, and fears. Dwelling indefinitely on the past in the hope of uncovering some dark, deep secret or confirming a pet theory is a waste of time and a diversion from matters more deserving of our attention.

In a nutshell, if one takes "Everything happens for a reason" or "It was or wasn't meant to be" to mean anything beyond "Natural events in the present flow from natural events in the past," one makes needless assumptions (2, 5, and 6), puts an overly optimistic spin on the flow of history (3), or risks superfluous and indefinite investigation (4).

*A version of this article appeared in *Free Inquiry*, December 2005/January 2006, Volume 26, No. 1, pp. 59-60.

CHAPTER 5
Right and Wrong

An Overview

The Challenge

We live in a diverse world. Although we are all human beings, we differ remarkably in many ways. For centuries philosophers have been trying to figure out if, behind the diversity, we're bound by common rules for living and, if so, what they are. The branch of philosophy called *morality* or *ethics* is devoted to this task. In this branch philosophers ask what makes actions right (good, moral, ethical, just) and what makes actions wrong (evil, immoral, unethical, unjust). Some writers attribute different meanings to the terms morality and ethics (and moral and ethical) but in this chapter that isn't done. They are used as synonyms. Specialists in ethics are called moral theorists, ethicians, or ethicists. Their work covers three areas:

- In *Meta-Ethics* philosophers seek to clarify the origin of our notions of right and wrong, the meaning of moral terms (good, evil, right, duty, etc.), and the status of moral judgments (universal or relative).
- In *General Ethics (or Theoretical Ethics)* philosophers ask whether there is an objective rule or a series of rules - *A Moral Law* - that all of us have a duty to learn and follow and which enables us to distinguish between right and wrong and, if so, what the Moral Law says.
- In *Applied Ethics (or Practical Ethics)* philosophers ask what is right and wrong in a specific case. They take a proposed moral rule and try to figure out how it applies in the here and now. A subdivision of Applied Ethics is *professional ethics (or occupational ethics)*. This subdivision addresses

moral issues which surface in one's profession or occupation. Most professions and occupations are governed by a *moral code* and questions arise as to how to apply a code in a specific case and under what circumstances, if any, a practitioner may violate the moral code. (1)

In this chapter, in the *Overview* and the *Readings*, we'll touch on all three areas.

The Basic Positions

We'll approach morality by contrasting two standpoints, Relativism and Objectivism. The former holds that right and wrong differ because they reflect personal tastes or social conventions while the latter holds that right and wrong are uniform because they reflect a universally-binding rule of conduct.

Relativism

Subjectivism

Subjectivists in ethics hold the view that what we call right and wrong is a matter of individual taste. For a subjectivist, when you refer to an action as right, you mean that you like it or approve of it, and when you refer to an action as wrong, you mean that you don't like it or you don't approve of it. Others may disagree with your likes and dislikes so that actions which you deem right, they may deem wrong, and actions which you deem wrong, they may deem right. It's much like ice cream. You may like vanilla and I may like chocolate. Neither of us is mistaken; it's all a matter of personal taste. There is no standard of right and wrong beyond an individual's tastes. One advocate of this position is Bertrand Russell. He wrote:

> The theory which I have been advocating is a form of the doctrine which is called the "subjectivity" of values. This doctrine consists in maintaining that, if two men differ about values, there is not a disagreement as to any kind of truth, but a difference of taste. If one man says 'oysters are good' and another says 'I think they are bad,' we recognize that there is nothing to argue about. The theory in question holds that all differences as to values are of this sort... (2)

Russell is accurate to a point. There may be some actions which some people judge moral or immoral based on personal taste or feeling. For a person to wear tight or loose clothes in public, or to use or not to use foul language regularly, or to attend or not to attend a wake in a tee shirt, cutoffs, and flip flops, falls into this category. On the other hand, there are some actions which seem to invite an evaluation on criteria beyond a person's tastes and feelings. For a person to drive drunk or sober, or to steal or not to steal, or to poison or not to poison a water supply, falls into this category.

Cultural Relativism

Cultural Relativism is the theory that an action is right if it is customary in a given society and wrong if it isn't. If divorce is customary in a society, then those who divorce act morally. If divorce is not customary in a society, then those who divorce act immorally. If multiple wives are customary in a society, then a man who takes four wives acts morally. If multiple wives are not customary in a society, then a man who takes four wives acts immorally. As Ruth Benedict, an anthropologist, put it, "Morality differs in every society, and is a convenient term for socially approved habits." Under this theory, there is no standard for right and wrong beyond custom and, since customs differ from place to place, morality differs from place to place.

But does diversity in customs nullify the possibility of an objective, trans-cultural standard of behavior? James Rachels (1940-2004) argues that it does not. (4) Rachels sees a faulty argument underlying cultural relativism which he calls the "Cultural Differences Argument." The premise of the argument is that "Different cultures have different moral codes." The conclusion of the argument is "Therefore, there is no objective 'truth' in morality." Rachels points out that even if the premise is true, the conclusion need not follow. The premise concerns *what people believe* and from the mere fact that two cultures differ in their beliefs does not rule out the possibility that one is mistaken or both are mistaken. Rachels gives this example. Say that one culture believes that the earth is round but another believes that it is flat. May we conclude from this disagreement that there is no objective truth about the shape of the earth? Of course not. Similarly, if one culture believes in human sacrifice to appease the gods and another does not, we should not conclude that there can be no objective truth about human sacrifice. For Rachels, then, despite cultural diversity, it may still be possible to find a standard of right and wrong beyond custom that applies to all of us.

Objectivism

Objectivism in morality is the position that there is a basic rule which governs human conduct such that actions which follow this rule are right and actions which violate this rule are wrong. This rule is variously called the moral law, the natural law, the law of nature, the law of God, or God's law. Objectivism is opposed to Relativism. It therefore challenges the positions outlined above that right and wrong reflect the tastes of an individual (Subjectivism) or the customs of a society (Cultural Relativism).

Objectivists typically subscribe to the view that the moral law flows from human nature. It is the nature of humans to be rational and social seekers of happiness and humans are entitled to fulfill their nature. The moral law gives a green light to actions which enable us to fulfill our nature and a red light to those that don't. For instance, for an objectivist, it is moral to drive a car sober but immoral to drive a car drunk because sober driving is likely to protect oneself and others from needless harm, including injury and death, while drunk driving is not. It is important to note that objectivists distinguish between the moral law, prescribed by nature, and the civil law, prescribed by government. In Chapter 6: Government, with the help of Plato and Dr. Martin Luther King, Jr., we'll explore what happens when there is a conflict between the two.

The view that there is a moral law that all humans have a duty to learn and to follow has had many advocates over the centuries, including Marcus Tullius Cicero (106-43 BCE) in the ancient world, Thomas Aquinas (1225-1274 CE) in the medieval world, and John Locke (1632-1704 CE) in the modern world. Here are excerpts from their writings:

Cicero:
...(L)aw in the proper sense is right reason in harmony with nature. It is spread through the whole human community, unchanging and eternal, calling people to their duty by its commands and deterring them from wrong-doing by its prohibitions. ...(A)ll peoples at all times will be embraced by a single and eternal and unchangeable law... Whoever refuses to obey it will be turning his back on himself because he has denied his nature as a human being... (*Republic*, Book Three, 33)

Thomas Aquinas:
Now among all others, the rational creature is subject to Divine providence in the most excellent way, in so far as it partakes of a share of providence, by being provident both for itself and for others. Therefore it has a share of the Eternal Reason, by which it has a natural inclination to its

due act and end; and this participation of the eternal law in the rational creature is called the natural law... ...(T)he light of natural reason, by which we discern what is good and what is evil, which is the function of the natural law, is nothing else than an imprint on us of the Divine light. It is therefore evident that the natural law is nothing else than the rational creature's participation of the eternal law. (*Summa Theologica*, Part I of Second Part, Question XCI, Article 2)

John Locke:
Hence, the law of nature can be described as being the decree of the divine will discernible by the light of nature and indicating what is and what is not in conformity with rational nature, and for this very reason commanding or prohibiting (actions). (*Essays on the Law of Nature*, I)

The state of nature (i.e., society without a government) has a law of nature to govern it, which obliges every one; and reason, which is that law, teaches all mankind who will but consult it that, being all equal and independent, no one ought to harm another in his life, health, liberty, or possessions... (*The Second Treatise of Government*, Chapter II, "Of the State of Nature")

Let's turn now to the major objectivist moral theories.

Virtue Ethics

Say that you're driving late at night and suddenly you run out of gas. You had hoped to fill the tank earlier but you were running late for work. You're about two miles from the house of a friend, Allison. You phone Allison's cell to see if she will help you. She says that she'll be there within twenty minutes with a container of gas. Why did you phone her and not someone else? Because you know her to be a generous, helpful person. Because you know that she values her friends. In other words, you know her *habits*.

The first philosopher to emphasize the importance of habits to the moral life was Aristotle (384-322 BCE). In his *Nichomachean Ethics* Aristotle argues that a person who wishes to achieve the highest good – happiness or well-being (*eudaimonia* in Greek) – must strive to do good deeds on a daily basis until doing so is habitual. This takes time. As a person acquires "practical wisdom," she will learn that *moderation* - the *mean* between extremes – is the path to happiness (with some exceptions). For instance, at a meal, you will neither take a meager portion nor commit gluttony; instead, you will take an amount which sustains your health and energy. In exercise, you will neither do too little nor push yourself to exhaustion; instead, you will pursue a regimen which is appropriate to your age, weight, and health. In social life, you will neither be a hermit nor a busybody; instead, you will show courtesy to all and devotion to family and friends. In charity, you will neither give nothing nor an extravagant amount; instead, you will give what you can afford. Here is how Aristotle puts it:

> Virtue, then, is a state of character concerned with choice, lying in a mean, i.e. the mean relative to us, this being determined by a rational principle, and that principle by which the man of practical wisdom would determine it. Now it is a mean between two vices, that which depends on excess and that which depends on defect...(4)

Note that Aristotle does not give us an explicit "moral law" or a list of specific do's and don'ts or an appeal to religion for moral guidance. He advances a secular morality, one which urges us to fulfill our nature as rational and social seekers of happiness. His work had a powerful influence on moral theorists who came later, especially *Natural Law theorists*, including Thomas Aquinas, John Locke, and many others, and *Ethical Egoists*. (See below in this chapter for Ethical Egoism and see Chapter 6: Government for Locke.)

Aristotle's moral theory has merit. The good life requires good habits. On the other hand, people with good habits can still do wrong. They can be blinded by tradition, as were "virtuous" slave owners, or by duty, as were "virtuous" bishops who acquiesced in rape and "virtuous" U.S. Government officials who acquiesced in torture. As a logician might say, good habits are a necessary but not a sufficient condition of a moral life.

Divine Command Theory

If you hold that the moral law is *Obey God* or *Obey God's Law* or *Follow God's commands and prohibitions* or *Do what God commands and do not do what God forbids*, then you subscribe to Divine Command Theory. Most people who embrace this theory take it to affirm the following: 1) There is a God, 2) God is good, 3) God has revealed the moral law, and 4) In the afterlife, God will reward those who follow the moral law and punish those who don't.

Divine Command Theory is hugely popular around the world. Most followers of Christianity and Islam, for example, the world's two most popular religions, endorse it. On the other hand, followers of religions which don't recognize a God (or gods) or which marginalize the role of God (or gods) for morality, such as Buddhism, do not endorse it. One of the advantages of Divine Command Theory is that it seems to provide a strong incentive for us to be moral – an all-powerful, all-knowing, and all-good God will dispense justice after we die. The theory faces a variety of difficulties, however.

- The rational arguments aimed at proving the existence of God meet with a flurry of criticism. (See Chapter 2: Religion.)
- The problem of evil raises legitimate questions about the claim that God is good (if there is a God). (See Chapter 2: Religion)
- There are deep and persisting disagreements among groups which endorse Divine Command Theory as to exactly what God commands and forbids. For starters, there is no consensus on where to find God's law. Should we look to a scripture (if so, which one and which interpretation – literal, historical, or symbolic)? Or to a prophet (if so, which one)? Or to clergy (if so, which one)? Or to a sect (if so, which one)? Or to a church body (if so, which one)? Or to private revelation? Or to reason?

   Sharp differences over morality exist not only among followers of different religions but among followers of the same religion.

   For instance, Christian groups are at odds on many issues including birth control, divorce, plurality of spouses, abortion, homosexuality, same sex marriage, gambling, hastening death, life support technology, blood transfusions, faith healing, the status of women, embryonic stem cell research, and evolution, among others.

   Also, among Muslims, there is controversy over the interpretation of many parts of the Qur'an and the Hadith. (Muslims believe that the Qur'an is Allah's revelation to the Prophet Muhammad through the angel Gabriel and that the Hadith records the deeds and teachings of Muhammad and his companions.) For instance, the Qur'an says:

   I will cast terror into the hearts of those who disbelieve. Therefore strike off their heads and strike off every fingertip of them. Qur'an 8:12

And the Hadith proclaims:

> *The Messenger of Allah said: I have been commanded to fight against people so long as they do not declare that there is no God but Allah.* Muslim 1:30

Are these passages, which clearly seem to entreat the faithful to violence against non-believers, to be taken literally? (5) ISIS, the self-proclaimed Islamic State of Iraq and Syria, other *jihadists*, and a minority of Muslims around the world say "Yes!" Most Muslims say "No!" (6)

- There is no proof either of an afterlife or of a Last Judgment; these are faith-based beliefs. Moreover, the idea that an all-good God is capable of punishing people for eternity in Hell is under increasing scrutiny within the religious community. (7)
- If belief in God and God's law is the path to morality, those who subscribe to Divine Command Theory face the predicament of explaining how religious authorities who take their cue from God (or so they say) have endorsed or acquiesced in morally corrupt practices ranging from slavery to racism to misogyny to pedophilia.
- Divine Command Theory seems to imply that religious people have a corner on the market on morality. This is simply untrue. Moral standards are as high among the non-religious as among the religious and, in some cases, higher. On this issue, see *A Lesson from Scandinavia* in the Readings for this chapter (Right and Wrong) and *Unbelief and the Vote* in the Readings for the next chapter (Government). (8)

Kantian Ethics

Many influential moral theories prioritize happiness – one's own or others – as the focus of the moral life. They instruct us to pursue the course which is likely to maximize happiness for oneself or others. Immanuel Kant (1724-1804) begs to differ. Whether the act does or does not produce happiness or some other desired end is morally irrelevant to Kant. So, what makes an act moral for Kant? Let's turn to a (hopefully, hypothetical) story.

You have a life-long friend, Sherry, whose birthday is next week on Saturday. To show your affection for her, and to lift her spirits after a divorce, you quietly organize a surprise birthday party at a local restaurant. You reserve a party room, you order a cake, you invite twenty or so mutual friends, and you con Sherry to show up on the pretext that you'll treat her to a birthday drink. Saturday evening arrives. When Sherry shows up, you escort her to the party room where all the guests salute her by singing "Happy Birthday." Sherry is moved to tears. But, alas, as they finish, she takes ill and collapses. You phone 911, an ambulance arrives and rushes her to a nearby hospital, and you and your friends gather in the emergency room waiting area. A doctor appears with bad news – Sherry has died from a heart attack. You are distraught.

If your moral grade is determined by the outcome of your surprise party, you get an F. "But, wait a minute," Kant says, "despite the result, you get an A because you acted from a *good will.* You had a *good intention.*" What exactly does he mean? Kant recognizes that we are rational and social animals. When we face a choice and lean toward a particular action, we need to ask ourselves if this action is one that we can endorse for all other people in similar circumstances to take. If we can, it gets the Kantian green light. If we can't, it doesn't.

Kant's term for the moral law is the *categorical imperative.* Categorical means absolute or unconditional and imperative means law or command. According to Kant, the categorical imperative is this: *Act only on a maxim that you can wish to universalize.* By maxim he means a rule covering an act that you're considering. By universalize he means to endorse it for everyone, not just yourself.

Kant gives four examples to clarify the application of the categorical imperative in his *Fundamental Principles of the Metaphysics of Morals*, published in 1785. Here's one that deals with a loan. Say that you need a loan but the person who can afford to give it to you will only do so if you promise to repay it by a certain date. But this date is unrealistic; you can't possibly meet it. Should you take the loan? According to Kant, the maxim covering this situation is *for the sake of personal gain, I will make a promise that I don't intend to keep.* Now, can you endorse this maxim as a rule for everyone to follow? No. If you did, promises would no longer be promises and people would "ridicule" promises "as vain pretences (sic)," according to Kant. Since you cannot universalize the maxim, you should not take the loan.

Let's use another example. (Kant isn't the source of this one.) Suppose a college student, Matt, is facing a final exam in a course that he needs to pass to complete his program. Right now he's on the borderline between a D and an F. Matt has a friend, Sarah, who works in the campus copy center where Matt's professor has her tests copied a week or so before she gives them. Sarah offers to give Matt a copy of the final. Should he accept? The maxim here is "If I have an opportunity to improve a test score by cheating, then I will do so." Can this be universalized? No. Authorizing everyone to cheat to improve a score on a test would invalidate tests. They would cease to be an accurate and reliable measure of knowledge and skill. This includes tests taken by attorneys, physicians, teachers, pilots, dietitians, nurses, pharmacists, mechanics, police officers, and countless others. No one could trust the claimed credentials of people on whom they rely. Who would wish to live in such a society? Since Matt cannot universalize the maxim, he should decline Sarah's offer.

Another version of the categorical imperative which Kant gives us is: *Always treat a human person as an end and never as a means only*. This one highlights the distinction between a person and a thing. A person is a conscious being with rights – entitlements – and feelings. This version entreats you to respect others and not use them simply as a tool of your convenience or pleasure. We do this in many ways – saying "thank you" or "have a good day," holding a door for another person, sending a birthday card or buying a gift for someone, apologizing for saying or doing something that we regret, tipping a server, complimenting a person, and so on.

In a modern service economy such as ours, however, it is sometimes difficult to treat a person as an end and not as a means. For instance, if you're ordering a Big Mac at McDonald's in the drive through lane, you use the voice which greets you as a means to a hamburger. You're not much concerned with him or her as a person. Perhaps she has just gone through a bankruptcy or lost a close friend to cancer. You have no desire to know such things or to commiserate with her. You're hungry and you want your Big Mac – period!

Aside from this, Kant's moral theory has problems. Here are two:

- Despite Kant's stated intention to prioritize one's intention (*a good will, a good motive, regard for duty*) and to marginalize results, his own examples rely on results. Of the four examples that he uses in the *Fundamental Principles of the Metaphysics of Morals*, you can make a case that he decides the morality of all four (suicide, false promise, squandering talent, and helping the poor) with a consideration of likely results.
- Kant's moral theory requires you to identify a maxim and figure out whether it can be universalized. The problem is that some situations lend themselves to multiple, and possibly contradictory, maxims. For instance,

say that you are a comptroller of a company and the CEO orders you to file a quarterly report to the Board of Directors that shows a more favorable financial picture than the actual one. The CEO has the authority to hire and fire. Your spouse lost her job last month, you're two months behind in your mortgage payments, and you have huge legal bills over a recent DUI. Landing a new job with comparable salary and benefits will be very difficult. What is the maxim here? Here are some plausible ones: "If I need to comply with an order from a superior to which I object to keep my job, then I will do so," "If I need to comply with an order from a superior to which I object to support my family and to pay my bills, then I will do so," "If I need to tell a lie in order to keep my job, then I will refuse to do so," and "If I need to violate the standards of my profession to please my superior, then I will refuse to do so." Perhaps you can come up with others. Which of these maxims is the one that Kant would cite? Which of them can and cannot be universalized? It's hard to tell. The point is that Kant's moral theory is vague and doesn't give one the guidance that one would like.

Utilitarian Ethics

One moral theory, Utilitarianism, is founded on the conception of human beings as rational and social seekers of happiness. Jeremy Bentham (1748-1832) and John Stuart Mill (1806-1873), both British, popularized this theory through their writings and, in Bentham's case, his proposals for social reform. When we make a choice, Utilitarianism encourages us to pursue the course of action that is the most *useful*, that is, the one that is likely to produce the most happiness (or pleasure). Thus we have the *Greatest Happiness Principle*, the GHP. Mill writes:

> The creed which accepts as the foundation of morals 'utility' or the 'greatest happiness principle' holds that actions are right in proportion as they tend to promote happiness; wrong as they tend to produce the reverse of happiness. By happiness is intended pleasure and the absence of pain; by unhappiness, pain and the privation of pleasure. (9)

When Utilitarians use the terms happiness and pleasure, they recognize distinctions. They recognize the *quantity* (more or less) and *quality* (mental and physical) of pleasures and the difference between *short-term* (immediate) and *long-term* (enduring) pleasures. The most "desirable and valuable" pleasures, Mill insists, are long-term, mental ones. We know this, Mill argues, because this is the verdict of virtually everyone who has experience of both types of pleasures. Mill writes:

> Now it is an unquestionable fact that those who are equally acquainted with and equally capable of appreciating and enjoying both do give a most marked preference to the manner of existence which employs their higher faculties. (10)

One additional point is important. In calculating pleasure, a person should seek the greatest sum. On occasion, this may require her to perform an action which benefits many but not herself. Mill writes that the standard of happiness for Utilitarians is "...not the agent's own happiness, but the greatest amount of happiness altogether..." (11)

Let's try to clarify these points with the help of examples.

1. Angeline, a Ph.D. in chemistry, is invited to join a cancer research project which is led by an internationally acclaimed scientist who is a Nobel laureate and which is supported by grants exceeding $100 million. If she accepts the offer, she will have to leave her current job as a university professor, which she enjoys, and say good-bye to her colleagues, her students, and her friends. If Angeline is a Utilitarian, what does she do? In my opinion, she changes jobs. Why? In the new post she has an opportunity to benefit far more people than she can in her current post. While it is true that she'll likely meet new colleagues, expand her knowledge, make new friends, and do exciting, invigorating, and rewarding work, the prospect of curing cancer and saving literally hundreds of millions of lives across the planet is the overriding factor.

2. Alex and Sharon are co-workers. Although both are married with children, they have an affair. After a month or so, they discuss their relationship. If Alex and Sharon are Utilitarians, what do they do? Again, in my opinion, they break off the affair. If they continue, it will harm them, their spouses, and their children. As time passes, they reason, the sexual excitement will wane, they will feel guilty, their secret will surface, and their spouses and children will be devastated.

Utilitarianism prompts several comments, among them:

- Utilitarianism predicates morality on anticipating the future but this is risky. As Scottish poet Robert Burns (1759-1796) wrote, "The best laid plans of mice and men often go astray." (See the story about Sherry above in *Kantian Ethics*.) There are contingencies down the road that are difficult, perhaps impossible, to anticipate. Often, hoped-for results don't materialize. Perhaps, morally speaking, Kant is right; intentions are more important than results.

- The GHP, like Kant's categorical imperative, is difficult to put into practice at times. Say that you're considering three courses of action. As best you can predict, one provides *a modest benefit for most people but none for you or anyone else*; another provides *a significant benefit for you and a few others but none for anyone else*; and yet another provides *a significant benefit for you and a modest benefit for a few others but none for anyone else*. If you're a Utilitarian, which course should you choose? It's difficult to say. (To complicate matters, we could calculate anticipated harm to self and others in each of the three courses.)

- Another difficulty with the GHP is this. In calculating "the greatest amount of happiness altogether," what does "altogether" mean? Whose happiness should you seek? Say that you're a parent with children. The Christmas season, with gift-giving, is near at hand. Should you buy gifts only for your children? How about children in impoverished families? Should you cut down on spending for your children and divert monies to them? Or, say that your car is eight years old and has over 100,000 miles. Do you buy a new one? Or do you keep the old one and make a sizeable donation to a charity which distributes food in poor African villages where malnutrition is rampant? What does the GHP require of you in these cases? If it requires you to defer your own happiness or the happiness of your family for the benefit of strangers, it is a deeply flawed moral theory, according to Ethical Egoists, to whom we now turn our attention.

Ethical Egoism

Among the sayings that we hear now and then are these: "Don't be a doormat," "Charity begins at home," and "Stand up for yourself." (12) If we convert these into a full-blown moral theory, it is Ethical Egoism. (Egoism derives from the Latin term, *ego*, which means I or self.) Ethical Egoism affirms that you should always seek your own long-term happiness (pleasure, benefit, gain, fulfillment, growth, flourishing, well-being, development, welfare, interest). With roots in Aristotle, it emphasizes that you are entitled to fulfill your nature, to develop your potential, to satisfy your needs. As with Utilitarianism, it recognizes that you are a rational and social seeker of happiness, that enduring pleasures are superior to immediate ones, that your needs are physical and mental, and that anticipated results are vital. Ethical Egoism parts the way with Utilitarianism, however, on the issue of priorities. Ethical Egoism prioritizes your own happiness; Utilitarianism prioritizes the sum total of happiness. Despite this, the gap between the two theories in practice is not as wide as one would suspect. This is because, in many cases, the action which benefits self also benefits others.

Ethical Egoism was first popularized in the United States by Russian-born Ayn Rand (1905-1982), a screenwriter, novelist, and philosopher, who called her philosophy *Objectivism*. In her novels, including *The Fountainhead* (1943) and *Atlas Shrugged* (1957), both of which were made into movies, Rand promoted the pursuit of rational self-interest. She considered altruism (from the Latin term *alter*, which means other or another) her chief enemy. "Altruism," she wrote, "declares that any action taken for the benefit of others is good, and any action taken for one's own benefit is evil." (13) By contrast, she insisted that, "...the actor must always be the beneficiary of his action and...must act for his own *rational* self-interest." (14)

Disciples of Rand, such as philosopher Tara Smith (b. 1961), have written extensively to interpret and develop Rand's work. One of the points that Smith emphasizes is that self-interest encompasses the whole self. A person has both "material" and "non-material" (or "spiritual") needs. For a fulfilling life, we need not only food, shelter, clothing, and medical care but much more. On this point Smith writes:

> A person's spiritual condition is also critical to his interest because it affects his enjoyment of life. Consciousness affords many of life's most sublime satisfactions. For many people, it is not exclusively physical pleasures – the prospect of another bowl of cereal or a warm fire (or even of fine champagne or terrific sex) – that animate the will to live. It is the drive to create, to understand, to solve challenging problems, to experience beauty, love, passion –in short, to engage and savor intellectually and emotionally. (15)

So, for an ethical egoist, a happy life will be marked by such things as good friends, challenging and satisfying work, enjoyment of the arts, pride in one's accomplishments, and respect, love, and companionship.

Is Ethical Egoism a sound theory? In my judgment, on balance, it has more strengths than weaknesses. Consider these points:

- The emphasis of Ethical Egoism on long-term happiness is a welcome one in today's world. A great many people fail to integrate the long view into their lives and careers. (See "Hedonism" below in this chapter.) They drop out of school, abuse alcohol and drugs, join gangs, reproduce prematurely (and often), lie, commit adultery, act irresponsibly in public, cancel appearances, miss work and class regularly, violate probation, and assume, wrongly, that secrets will remain secrets. Many damage their lives and careers irreparably. Some crash and burn. Even if Ethical Egoism never catches on across the globe, civilization would be a better place with the infusion of a strong dose of prudence.

- Ethical Egoism is a favorite target of clergy and others who argue that a moral person is selfless. Many clergy tell us that God's people, the ones who shall "inherit the kingdom of God," must live to serve others, not themselves. They must put the needs of others ahead of their own and be their neighbor's keeper. Two points are relevant. Firstly, one can serve self and others simultaneously. It's called reciprocity. Anyone who provides a good or a service for pay does it. Secondly, the indictment of Ethical Egoism by clergy is motivated, ironically, by an appeal to self-interest. Why, we may ask, should we serve others? Why should we be altruists and not egoists? Why should we be our neighbor's keeper? Answer: *To save our souls! To go to Heaven!* Religious morality is simply Ethical Egoism plus these faith-based beliefs: there is a God who reveals a moral law and who will reward those who obey it and punish those who don't at the Final Judgment. In essence, believers sacrifice for others in this life to secure happiness for themselves in the next one.

- Ethical Egoism carries the same liability as Utilitarianism. It requires us to anticipate the future, a risky enterprise. One can seldom be certain that the future will unfold as we expect. The same lesson that we mentioned above about Utilitarianism applies here. Isn't one's intention important? If you organize a block watch in your neighborhood after a series of burglaries, but crimes continue, your intention to reduce crime, though unfulfilled, has moral worth. If you expand your business and employ twenty new employees, but one of them suffers a fatal injury in a fall from a catwalk, are you a moral monster? I don't think so.

- Ethical Egoism is a demanding moral theory. If you want a happy, fulfilling life, you must adopt a life style and cultivate habits that promote one. You will exercise regularly, eat and drink in moderation, avoid substance abuse, strive for stable personal relationships, develop good friends, avoid scandals, avoid trouble with the law, honor your contracts and promises, stay informed, exercise thrift, defer gratification regularly, perform your job well, support activities near and far that benefit you directly or indirectly, and drive cars, take vacations, wear clothes, and pursue hobbies that you can afford. And this is only part of the agenda. To be a successful ethical egoist, you need self-discipline and prudence.

Hedonism

It is essential that you understand the difference between Ethical Egoism and Hedonism. (Hedonism derives from the Greek for delight or pleasure.) Ethical Egoists take the long view when it comes to pleasure and they seek the full gamut of mental and physical pleasures. By contrast, hedonists take the short view when it comes to pleasure and they focus on physical pleasures such as sex, eating, and getting high. Often hedonists become addicted to such pleasures to the exclusion of all other aspects of living. They live from hour to hour and day to day with little thought of the future. So dedicated are they to pleasure that many will steal, lie, and cheat, if necessary, to pursue it. Hedonism was portrayed well in a 1966 British film, *Alfie*, starring Michael Caine as Alfie. Alfie was so obsessed with sex that his life revolved around affairs, usually of short duration, with both single and married women. They were his "birds," mere things which he used and discarded. He was incapable of sustaining a relationship as he gallivanted on the sexual merry-go-round. Finally, after dozens and dozens of flings, Alfie finally realized that his self-indulgence had deprived him of the happiness that comes with commitment, love, and mutual respect. (16)

One can make the case that hedonists should not even be mentioned in a discussion of morality. After all, they don't reflect on right and wrong at all. The quest for pleasure defines their existence. In a variation of Descartes, they affirm "I get it on, therefore I exist." Yet, implicitly, hedonists embrace a morality. Their "good" is pleasure – the sooner, the better: their "evil" is pain or the absence of pleasure. As Alfie found out, however, his frivolous life style led to disappointment, despair, even self-loathing. Sooner or later hedonists ask in desperation: "Is this all there is?" Indeed, a lyric in the song for the film *Alfie* sung by Cher is "Is that all there is, Alfie?" And, of course, for hedonists, the answer is "Yes." The experience of Alfie and other hedonists sends us several signals:

- pleasure is not commensurate with happiness,
- a fulfilling life requires one to look beyond the short-term,
- treating others simply as instruments of one's own pleasure or convenience backfires eventually, and
- developing mutual trust and respect in one's dealings with others is essential to one's own psychological health.

Ethical Intuitionism

The Objectivist moral theories which we have examined thus far all involve the use of reason. Ethical Intuitionism is the exception to the rule. It is an Objectivist moral theory but it does not seek right and wrong by reasoning. Instead, Ethical Intuitionism affirms that you and I have intuitions – flashes of insight – about right and wrong. Once the facts of a situation are clear to us, we immediately sense what we should and should not do.

One advocate of Ethical Intuitionism is novelist-philosopher William Gass (1924-2017). He tells this story:

Imagine I approach a stranger on the street and say to him, 'If you please, sir, I desire to perform an experiment with your aid.' The stranger is obliging, and I lead him away. In a dark place conveniently by, I strike his head with the broad of an axe and cart him home. I place him, buttered and trussed, in an ample electric oven. The thermostat reads 450 degrees Fahrenheit. Thereupon I go off to play poker with friends and forget all about the obliging stranger in the stove. When I return, I realize I have overbaked my specimen, and the experiment, alas, is ruined. (17)

Gass' point is that as soon as you understand what he did to the obliging stranger, you instantly condemn it. You don't have to figure out if the action is the mean between extremes; or if God commands or forbids it; or if it is covered by a maxim which you can universalize; or if it benefits a lot of people; or if it benefits Gass. The "experiment' is an example of what Gass calls a "clear case." In such cases, you have a moral intuition which informs you that the "experiment" was horrid, cruel, and despicable. You need not appeal to moral principles, although sometimes moral principles validate your moral intuitions. For instance, an ethical egoist might observe that what Gass did to the obliging stranger is immoral because it has harmful consequences for him. He will be arrested, tried, convicted, and punished, possibly with death. For Gass, what the ethical Egoist says about the "experiment" is true. But that is not what makes it evil. We grasp that it is evil even if we have never heard of Ethical Egoism because this is how we are; this is how we tick. We have an inborn *moral sense* which, like a traffic signal, tells us to go (green) or to stop (red). Some call it *conscience*. Finally, Gass observes, "...(N)o more convincing refutation of any ethic could be given than by showing that it approved of my baking the obliging stranger." (18)

Ethical Intuitionism presents us with several problems. Probably the most serious one is that it fails to account for moral disagreement. If humans were engineered to produce uniform moral insights, how do we explain the strong differences over moral issues that exist? One suspects that moral intuitions differ so much because they reflect enculturation – social conditioning. Most people in pre-civil war America had strong moral intuitions that slavery was morally permissible. Today we don't. Tens of millions of men and women in Islamic countries have strong moral intuitions that men, but not women, may have multiple spouses, and that men, but not women, may pursue education and careers. People in most non-Islamic nations don't. Faith healers have strong moral intuitions that they should pray over their sick children. Moral intuitions send the rest of us to a physician. Thus, while some cases may prompt uniform moral intuitions, many do not. In the United States, there certainly are not uniform moral intuitions about abortion, contraception, premarital sex, homosexuality, divorce, euthanasia, use of cell phones while driving, legalization of marijuana and other drugs, the status of women, the moral status of animals, prayer in the schools, religious symbols on public property, public funding of religious charities, and the functions of government, among others. Accordingly, investigation, discussion, and debate are necessary and unavoidable. So, moral theories are not going away any time soon.

Footnotes:

1. General Ethics and Applied Ethics make up *Normative Ethics*.
2. Bertrand Russell, *Science and Religion*, Oxford University Press, 1997, pp. 237-238.
3. See James Rachels, *The Elements of Moral Philosophy*, Fourth Edition, McGraw-Hill, 2003. See especially Chapter 2, "The Challenge of Cultural Relativism," pp. 16-31, from which these quotes are taken.
4. From *The Basic Works of Aristotle*, edited with an introduction by Richard McKeon, Random House, 1941, p. 959.
5. For additional passages from the Qur'an and the Hadith which promote violence, see www.thereligionof peace.com/quran/023-violence.htm.
6. On Muslim opinion world-wide about the propriety of violence against non-believers, see www.religionofpeace.com/pages/opinion-polls.htm
7. See Rob Bell, *Love Wins*, HarperOne, 2011. Bell writes:

    > A staggering number of people have been taught that a select few Christians will spend forever in a peaceful, joyous place called heaven, while the rest of humanity spends forever in torment and punishment in hell with no chance for anything better... This is misguided and toxic and ultimately subverts the contagious spread of Jesus's message of love, peace, forgiveness, and joy that our world desperately needs to hear. *Preface*, viii. Also see p. 95.

8. For an argument that religion produces moral ambiguity, see Ronald A. Lindsay, "Religious Morality: Pointless, Worthless, and Utterly Subjective," *Free Inquiry*, December 2014/January 2015, pp. 4-6.
9. John Stuart Mill, *Utilitarianism*, Library of Liberal Arts, 1957, p. 10. (Originally published in 1863)
10. *Ibid*, p. 12.
11. *Ibid.*, pp. 15-16.
12. These are mentioned in Tara Smith, *Viable Values: A Study of Life as the Root and Reward of Morality*, Rowman & Littlefield, 2002, p. 155.
13. Ayn Rand, *The Virtue of Selfishness*, Signet Books, 1964, p. viii.
14. *Ibid.*, p. x.
15. Smith, *Viable Values...*, p. 161.
16. A discovery similar to Alfie's was made by Cheryl Strayed who fell into a self-destructive chapter in her life after the death of her forty-five year old mother due to lung cancer. To extract herself from a life of heroin, alcohol, and sexual indulgence, Strayed took a 1,100 mile solo hike over

the Pacific Crest Trail in 1995 at age twenty-six. She recounts her life struggles and her hike in her book *Wild: From Last to First on the Pacific Crest Trail*, Knopf, 2012. The film version, "Wild," starring Reese Witherspoon, was released in December, 2014.

17. William Gass, *Philosophical Review*, LXVI (1957), pp. 193-204.

18. *Ibid.*

Recommendations for Further Study:

1. Peter Singer, *Practical Ethics*, Third Edition, Cambridge University Press, 2011.
2. Andrew I. Cohen and Christopher Heath Wellman, Editors, *Contemporary Debates in Applied Ethics*, Blackwell Publishing, 2005.
3. G. E. Moore, *Principia Ethica*, Cambridge University Press, 1903.
4. Michael Huemer, *Ethical Intuitionism*, Palgrave Macmillan, 2005.
5. C. L. Stevenson, *Facts and Values*, Yale University Press, 1963.
6. Richard Brandt, *Ethical Theory*, Prentice Hall, 1959.
7. Bertrand Russell, *Religion and Science*, Oxford University Press, 1997.
8. John Stuart Mill, *Utilitarianism*, many editions.
9. Tara Smith, *Viable Values: A Study of Life as the Root and Reward of Morality*, Rowman & Littlefield, 2000.
10. Kai Nielsen, *Ethics Without God*, Pemberton Books, 1973.
11. Ayn Rand, *The Virtue of Selfishness*, Signet Books, 1964.
12. Tibor R. Machan, *Ayn Rand*, Peter Lang, 1999.
13. James A. Haught, *2000 Years of Disbelief: Famous People with the Courage to Doubt*, Prometheus Books, 1996.
14. James A. Haught, *Holy Horrors: An Illustrated History of Religious Murder and Madness*, Prometheus Books, 1990.
15. Immanuel Kant, *The Foundations of Metaphysics of Morals*, 1785, many editions.
16. James Rachels, *The Elements of Moral Philosophy*, Fourth Edition, McGraw-Hill, 2003.
17. Paul Kurtz, *Exuberance: A Philosophy of Happiness*, Prometheus Books, 1977.
18. Paul Kurtz, *Eupraxophy: Living Without Religion*, Prometheus Books, 1989.
19. Paul Kurtz, *Forbidden Fruit: The Ethics of Humanism*, Prometheus Books, 1988.
20. Paul Kurtz, *Embracing the Power of Humanism*, Rowman & Littlefield Publishers, Inc., 2000.
21. Robert G. Olson, *Ethics: A Short Introduction*, Random House, 1978.
22. Robert G. Olson, *The Morality of Self-Interest*, Harcourt, Brace & World, 1956.
23. Richard Taylor, *Virtue Ethics: An Introduction*, Linden Books, 1991.
24. J.J.C. Smart and Bernard Williams, *Utilitarianism: For & Against*, Cambridge University Press, 1973.
25. Peter J. Gomes, *The Good Book: Reading the Bible With Mind and Heart*, HarperSanFrancisco, 2002.
26. Margaret Pabst Battin, *Ethical Issues in Suicide*, Prentice-Hall, 1995.
27. Margaret Pabst Battin, *The Least Worst Death: Essays in Bioethics on the End of Life*, Oxford University Press, 1994.
28. Walter Glannon, *Biomedical Ethics*, Oxford University Press, 2005.
29. Rob Bell, *Love Wins*, HarperOne, 2011.

30. Jennifer Michael Hecht, *Stay: A History of Suicide and the Philosophies Against It*, Yale University Press, 2013.

31. Tom Flynn, "Less Secular Than It Seems," *Free Inquiry*, April/May, 2014, pp. 56-60.

32. Jose Luis Perez Trivino, *The Challenges of Modern Sport to Ethics: From Doping to Cyborgs*, Lexington Books, 2013.

33. Susan Jacoby, *Never Say Die: The Myth and Marketing of The New Old Age*, Pantheon Books, 2011.

34. Cheryl Strayed, *Wild: From Lost to Found on the Pacific Crest Trail*, Knopf, 2012.

35. Susan Wolf, *Meaning in Life and Why It Matters*, Princeton University Press, 2010.

36. Annie Laurie Gaylor, *Woe to the Women, The Bible Tells Me So: The Bible, Female Sexuality & the Law*, Freedom From Religion Foundation, 2004.

Readings: Right and Wrong

A Lesson from Scandinavia

Tom Shipka (2008)

During the years 2005 and 2006, American sociologist Phil Zuckerman spent fourteen months in Denmark and Sweden to study these two societies. In a recent book, he reports these findings. (1)

- Denmark and Sweden have among the lowest rates of violent crime in the world. (pp. 28-29) (2)
- Denmark and Sweden have the lowest rates of HIV and AIDS in the world. (p. 27)
- Sweden is third and Denmark is fifth in the world in economic competitiveness. (p. 27)
- On gender equality, Denmark is second and Sweden is third in the world. (p. 27)
- On access to the Internet, Sweden is third and Denmark is fourth in the world. (p. 28)
- Denmark and Sweden are tied for the lowest infant mortality rates in the world with Norway, Iceland, Japan, and Singapore. (p. 26)
- Denmark and Sweden are tied for first place with the Netherlands in the health and safety of children. (p. 26)
- Denmark ranks fourth and Sweden ranks eighth in the world in the standard of living. (p. 27)
- Political corruption is virtually non-existent in Denmark and Sweden. (p. 28)
- Denmark and Sweden are tied for first in the world in a recent international study of social justice (p. 30) (3), and
- Denmark ranks second and Sweden ranks third in the world in financial aid to poor nations. (p. 29)

Thus, according to Zuckerman, Danes and Swedes are among the most contented and generous people on the planet. But that's not all that Zuckerman has to report about these two nations. Remarkably, he notes, two of the most prosperous societies in the world are also two of the least religious. (4) Indeed, a huge majority in both countries are atheists or agnostics. Only 24% of Danes and 16%

of Swedes believe in a personal God compared to more than 90% in the United States. (p. 24) Only 18% of Danes and 33% of Swedes believe in heaven compared to 80% of Americans. Only 10% of Danes and Swedes believe in hell compared to 75% of Americans. (p. 11, pp. 24-25) This is the lowest rate of belief in hell in the entire world! (p. 25) Next, only 7% of Danes and 3% of Swedes believe that the Bible is the literal word of God compared to 33% in the United States. (p. 25) Further, Danes and Swedes have the lowest church attendance in the world with only 3% of Danes and 7% of Swedes attending regularly. (p. 25, p. 162) (5) Also, only 8% of Danes and 15% of Swedes consider it important for a politician to believe in God compared to 64% of Americans who do (p. 12), and contrary to public and private practice in America, very few Danes and Swedes pray. (p. 2) Finally, more than 80% of Danes and Swedes accept evolution while less than half our population does. (p. 10) (6)

Professor Zuckerman sees an important lesson for us in his study of Denmark and Sweden. Contrary to what we've heard from "certain outspoken conservative Christians" (7), the sociologist suggests, a secular society need not be a scene of violence and depravity. (p. 4, pp. 17-18) Denmark and Sweden, he says, are not only "impressive models of societal health" (p. 17) but living proof that humans can survive and prosper without religion. (pp. 55-56) (8)

1. Zuckerman reports his findings in *Society without God: What the Least Religious Nations Can Tell Us About Contentment*, New York University Press, 2008. All references hereinafter are to page numbers of this book.

2. For instance, in Aarhus, Denmark, a city of 250,000 residents, there was a total of one murder in 2004. (p. 6)

3. This study was done by a German group of social scientists associated with an institute called Hans-Bocker Stiftung. (p. 30) Denmark and Sweden are not without problems, however. Taxes are high, there is social friction due to recent waves of immigration, children eat too much candy, rates of bicycle thefts are high, fertility rates are low, and alcohol consumption is high. (p. 34)

4. Other irreligious societies are the Netherlands, the Czech Republic, South Korea, Estonia, France, Japan, Bulgaria, Norway, England, Scotland, Wales, Hungary, and Belgium. (p. 25) Zuckerman points out that in all of these relatively secular societies the citizens freely gravitated from a religious to an irreligious perspective unlike North Korea, the former Soviet Union, China, and Albania where the governments attempted to impose secularism on the citizens. Zuckerman says that forced secularism doesn't work. See pp. 20-22.

5. Paradoxically, despite the fact that most Danes and Swedes are atheists or agnostics and don't attend church regularly, 83% of Danes and 80% of Swedes continue voluntarily to pay a tax to the National Church, which is Lutheran (p. 112), and many hold traditional events such as weddings, baptisms, confirmations, and funerals in church. Zuckerman says that Danes and Swedes, while rejecting the supernatural dimensions of Christianity - Jesus performed miracles, Jesus was God, Jesus rose from the dead, the Bible is God's revelation, the Genesis account of creation is accurate, there is an afterlife with a heaven and a hell, etc. – maintain a "cultural religion" similar to many Jews. (pp. 153-155) Oddly, in Denmark a person may be a pastor and an atheist. (p. 154)

6. Despite the fact that Danes and Swedes are irreligious, they are not hostile to religion, they shun serious discussions of it, they deem a person's views about religion a private matter, and many non-believers dislike being labeled an atheist because they take the term to imply hostility to religion. Further, many non-believers self-identify as "Christians." When one asks them what it means to be a Christian, they say it means being kind, helping people who need help, not hurting others, etc. As a rule they reject the supernatural components. See Chapter 8, "Cultural Religion," pp. 150-166. Also, see pp. 97-109.

7. Zuckerman lists the following examples of Christian conservatives who claim that a society that is irreligious will fail: Pat Robertson, the late Jerry Falwell, Ann Coulter, Bill O'Reilly, Laura Schlesinger, William Bennett, Rush Limbaugh, and Paul Weyrich. (p. 4, pp. 17-18)

8. American fundamentalists will no doubt object to Zuckerman's strongly favorable evaluation of Denmark and Sweden by noting that in these countries abortion has been legal for more than thirty years, prostitution is legal, and homosexuality is tolerated.

Self-Interest

Tom Shipka (2006)

Many say that to be moral a person must be an altruist, one who puts the interests of others ahead of one's own. A philosophical movement in the twentieth-century called Objectivism, led by novelist-philosopher Ayn Rand, challenged this and proposed that to be moral a person should put the interests of self ahead of the interests of others. Rand, an advocate of ethical egoism, argued that human beings have a moral duty to promote their own long-term self-interest (or self-fulfillment or happiness). Rand's new proposal evoked strong criticism from many philosophers and religious leaders who accused Rand of abandoning ethics altogether.

While there may be shortcomings in ethical egoism, the idea that it prioritizes self-interest, is, in my view, not one of them. The critics of ethical egoism, I believe, have a superficial and simplistic understanding of what self-interest entails. It certainly does not entail a self-indulgent hedonism, living solely for the pleasures of the moment. And it certainly does not isolate the individual from others or authorize the individual to manipulate others or to ignore their right to their own happiness. Let's reflect on these points.

Genuine self-interest rules out self-indulgent hedonism. A person who seeks his or her own happiness in life is required to exercise self-restraint and moderation, to defer gratification, and to take into account long-term and not merely short-term consequences. Imagine, if you will, two people. Let's call them Jack and Jill. Jack is obese and never exercises while Jill has a balanced diet and goes to the gym three times a week. Jack routinely drinks himself into a near coma and lost his driver's license after a third DUI while Jill drinks moderately. Jack dropped out of high school, works sporadically, and has filed bankruptcy twice while Jill worked her way through college, eventually completed a master's in accounting, and now leads her own solvent and growing CPA firm. Which individual is more genuinely self-interested? Is it the self-indulgent, undisciplined Jack or the self-restrained, disciplined Jill? I would argue that it is Jill.

Next, ethical egoists recognize that their own happiness is contingent on successful, mutually beneficial relationships with family, friends, business associates, and others. They recognize that their own happiness is served by earning and preserving friendship, trust, respect, and even love in many cases. Back to Jack and Jill. Jack is a loner who has few friends and a history of short-lived romances. On the other hand, Jill has a large circle of friends and has been with the same partner for a dozen years. Jack routinely stretches the truth and breaks promises, and seldom helps others, while Jill strives to tell the truth and to keep her promises, and her friends know that they can count on her in a pinch. Again, which individual is more genuinely self-interested? I would argue that it is Jill. Jill understands that her psychological, social, and economic well-being are linked to enduring relationships with people who come to value her. Indeed, one key source of her own happiness is being valued by others.

To the traditionally religious who speak disparagingly of self-interest, and demonize ethical egoists, I pose this question: Doesn't religion itself promote self-interest? Doesn't religion entreat people to save their souls so that they will enjoy eternal happiness?

The Right to Die

Tom Shipka (2005)

The Terry Shiavo case in Florida catapulted the issue of the right to die into national prominence in an unprecedented way. Millions of Americans are asking "Does a person have a right to die?" I believe that the answer is yes.

Two main arguments support the right of a person to die, one from autonomy, the other from compassion.

The argument from autonomy, or self-determination, holds that a person has the right to determine as much as possible the course of his or her life, dying is the last chapter in a person's life, and therefore a person has the right to determine as much as possible the circumstances of his or her dying.

The argument from compassion holds that a person is entitled to be spared suffering, protracted dying often involves considerable suffering, and therefore a dying person is entitled to hasten his or her death in order to end this suffering.

Those who propose such arguments almost always offer them in the context of several assumptions. These include the requirement that the person has been diagnosed as dying, that the person is a competent adult, that the person expresses his or her wishes about death in writing or verbally, and that the person is not under any pressure to hasten death by family members or others who may benefit in some way from the death.

There are many counter-arguments to the arguments supporting the right to die. I will mention two common ones.

Some say that only God has the right to terminate the life of a human being and that those who choose to die sooner rather than later are "playing God." But this point is not particularly helpful. In the case of Terry Schiavo, for instance, was keeping her alive in a persistent vegetative state assisting God's will or defying it? If your interpretation is that it was assisting God's will, that's fine, for you! Write your living will soon if you haven't already done so expressing your wish to be kept alive indefinitely by medical technology when there is no realistic prospect of recovery. But you do not have the right to speak for others who do not share your interpretation.

Others say that improvements in pain relief - palliation - enable doctors and organizations such as Hospice to take the sting out of dying. With morphine and other drugs they can substantially reduce pain so that a dying patient is spared the suffering and agony that we used to associate with many causes of death. Palliation will give the patient additional weeks or months of life relatively free of pain. The problem with this argument is two-fold. In the first place, palliation often diminishes mental acuity. I remember members of my own family whose morphine injections relieved pain but put them in a permanent fog for the rest of their days. In the second place, palliation does not alter the typical course of deterioration in which a dying person loses mobility, becomes confined to a bed permanently, loses control of his or her bowels, and becomes ever more dependent upon others and ever less dependent upon self. In other words, the side effect of palliation can be loss of self-reliance, pride, and dignity.

Debate over the right to die will continue in America, as it should. As it does, all of us should read, listen, and reflect. The stakes for each of us individually and for the nation as a whole are high. Meanwhile, if you don't have a living will, it's time to prepare one.

CHAPTER 6

Government

An Overview

Definitions

In this chapter we'll address three basic questions: Do we need a government? Do we have a moral duty to obey the government? What type of government is best? Before we can answer these questions, we need to clarify several terms, including government, law, power, authority, force, and economy.

- A *government* is an institution in society whose purpose is to make and enforce *laws* for the benefit of the people governed. In the modern world, there are three basic types of government – *democracy, dictatorship*, and *communism*.
- A *law*, according to St. Thomas Aquinas (1225-1274), is "an ordinance of reason for the common good, promulgated by him who has care of the community." (1) An ordinance is a rule or order. Notice that, according to Aquinas, these rules should be the product of reason, not emotion, and should aim at the benefit of the community at large, not a special interest. Notice also that they must be promulgated, that is, publicized. This is a problem in today's world because hundreds of new laws are enacted every year and most of us learn about only a small percentage of them. "(B)y him who has care of the community" is Aquinas' phrase for a legitimate authority, including a government.

- In order for a government to enact and to enforce laws, it must have *power*. To possess *power* is to control or influence others, even if they resist. Legitimate or morally justified power is called *authority*. Illegitimate or morally unjustified power is called *force* or *coercion*. Power accrues necessarily not only to government but to other social entities, including families, schools, companies, etc. It is sometimes debatable as to whether a particular exercise of power is an act of authority or force. For instance, say that a chief of police suspends an officer without pay for five days for showing up five minutes late for roll call on one occasion without inquiring why the officer was late. Authority or force? On the other hand, there are clear cases. For instance, a parent who disciplines a six-year old for misplacing the TV remote by severely beating her is exercising force, not authority.

- An *economy* (or an economic system) is an institution in society whose purpose is to produce and distribute goods and services to people. In the modern world, there are three main types of economies (*capitalism*, *socialism*, and a *mixed system*). Most modern economies are mixed systems which incorporate elements from both capitalism (e.g., property privately owned, free market controls production and distribution, private for-profit businesses, limited government services, private schools and colleges) and socialism (e.g., property publicly owned, government controls production and distribution, no private for-profit businesses, extensive government services, public schools and colleges).

The Flaws of Government

The flaws of government are well-known. Some governments, so-called *failed states*, are so weak that they cannot maintain order and protect life and property (e.g., Somalia). Although they're not called failed states, some governments fail to provide adequate help to citizens after a natural disaster (e.g., the United States after Hurricane Katrina struck the Gulf Coast) or cause financial crises by failing to regulate the financial sector (e.g., the U.S. in allowing the Wall Street "meltdown") or feud internally to a point of paralysis (e.g., the U.S. Congress during Barack Obama's second term) or botch the implementation of a new law or program (e.g., the U.S. with The Patient Protection and Affordable Care Act). Some governments are corrupt (e.g., Afghanistan and Iraq where hundreds of millions of dollars of U.S. aid is "unaccounted for"). Some governments are theocracies (e.g., Saudi

Arabia, where Islam dominates the society, women are subordinate, and apostasy – conversion from Islam to another religion – is punishable by death). Some governments accrue huge debts that they cannot pay and destabilize the world economy (e.g., Greece, Italy, Spain, Ireland, and Portugal). The list goes on and on.

Anarchism

Frustration and anger over the failures of government has led many times in history to a call for the abolition of government in favor of an alternative social experiment where voluntary associations take over the traditional functions of government. This proposal is called *anarchism* from the Greek words which mean "without a ruler" and its advocates are called *anarchists*. Should we take the proposal to abolish government seriously? Does it have merit? Or is it reckless pie-in-the-sky speculation, a utopian dream? While I regularly share the anarchist's frustration and anger over government, I nevertheless cast my vote for government over anarchism. Here are my reasons:

1. *In the modern world, there are no successful anarchist precedents.* Although there have been dozens of anarchist experiments - so-called utopian communities - in the United States, they all failed. Examples are Brook Farm, the Fruitlands, the Shakers, Pullman, Harmony, and the Diggers. All of these were agricultural except Pullman, which was a mix of farming and industry.

   Further, the challenges which the world's seven billion plus people face today are far more serious than those which the small, short-lived utopian communities faced in the past. They include overpopulation, global warming, energy alternatives to oil and gasoline, terrorism, AIDS, Ebola and other viruses, drug cartels, conflict within and among religions, access to medical care, the proliferation of nuclear weapons, and shortages of food, among others.

   If anarchist societies did not survive and prosper in the past facing modest challenges, why should we expect that they will survive and prosper in the future facing far more serious and complex challenges? Indeed, success in the future will require collaboration by the world's nation-states and possibly creation of a new, supra-national government.

2. *Voluntary associations, should they materialize, will eventually take on the trappings of government.* Members will assume roles, some as leaders, others

as followers. A decision-making process will be adopted. Policies, rules, projects, and goals will be set. If and when compliance is not voluntary, it will be forced. Enforcement means police, judges, and jails. Dissent and factions will surface. Traditional differences among people will remain - race, religion, education, language, customs, and others - fueling conflict. The financial burden will be shared. (This means the "T" word – taxes!) Finally, inept or corrupt individuals will sooner or later occupy some leadership positions. Thus, the new social organizations will be indistinguishable from governments.

The Law and Morality

Duty

If we assume – as I propose – that the prospects of living without a government are negligible and that government is here for the duration, the next issue is whether we have a *duty* (or obligation) to obey the laws, policies, and regulations which government adopts and, if we do, what *the nature of the duty* is.

Let's turn our attention, then, to duties. Here are three important points:

- Rights are *entitlements, just claims on others, what one is entitled to do.* Duties are *obligations, responsibilities, what one is expected to do.* Rights and duties are correlative, that is, they imply one another. For instance, if I have a right to life, you have duty not to murder me, and if you have a right to property, I have a duty not to steal from you.
- Some duties are *more basic* and *important* than others. The more basic and important ones take precedence over the less basic and important ones. For instance, say that a member of your family suddenly has severe chest pains and shortness of breath as you prepare to leave for work. Although you have a duty to be on time for work, your duty to help your sick relative is a more basic and important one.
- Many hold that some duties are so basic and important that we are never morally excused from complying with them. Such duties are called *absolute* or *unconditional* or *unqualified* duties in contrast to others which are called *relative* or *conditional* or *qualified* duties. If you have an absolute duty, no conditions could possibly arise which exempt you from compliance. On the other hand, if you have a conditional duty, conditions could possibly arise which exempt you from compliance. In the previous

example, it could be plausibly argued that your duty to help your sick relative (or your duty to save a life) is absolute while your duty to be on time for work is conditional.

If we do indeed have a duty to obey government, the fact is that a great many people routinely shirk it. Consider traffic laws. Many drivers exceed the posted speed limit, cruise through a stop sign, fail to yield to an oncoming vehicle, and make turns without using turn signals. Further, in a typical month in the United States, there are tens of thousands of crimes – murder, rape, burglary, sale and use of "controlled substances," shop lifting, identity theft, and dozens of others – many of which go unsolved and unpunished.

With this background, let's examine whether we have a duty to obey our government, and if we do, what sort of duty it is. To address this we enlist the help of the ancient Greek philosopher, Plato (424/423-348/347 BCE), and the twentieth-century civil rights leader, Dr. Martin Luther King, Jr. (1929-1968).

Plato and Dr. King agree on three important points:

- government is necessary,
- citizens should not use violence to change a law to which they object, and
- citizens have a duty to obey the law.

They differ, however, on the nature of this duty.

- Plato's position is that we have an absolute or unconditional or unqualified duty to obey the law; for Plato, to violate a law is always to act immorally; for Plato, no circumstances can possibly arise which exempt us from the duty to obey the law.
- Dr. King's position is that we have a relative or conditional or qualified duty to obey the law; for Dr. King, to violate a law is not always to act immorally; for Dr. King, circumstances can possibly arise which exempt us from the duty to obey the law.

Plato

Late in his life Socrates (469 BCE-399 BCE) was charged, tried, and convicted of two crimes – *impiety* and *corruption of youth*. The first was leveled by political enemies who claimed that he disrespected the gods of Athens, a charge unsupported by any known evidence. The second was prompted by his habit of encouraging young Athenians to shape their own beliefs and practices instead of being a slave to tradition. Having been found guilty, and facing death or banishment, he opted for death, rejecting banishment so that he would not be separated from the city, the family, and the friends that he loved. As he sat in his jail cell awaiting his execution, he had a visit from his long-time friend, Crito, who pleaded with Socrates to escape from jail and to flee to a distant place for his remaining years. Crito and others had hatched an escape plan and raised a pension to support Socrates after his escape. To accept Crito's offer to save his life, of course, would require Socrates to violate the law because he had been charged, tried, convicted, and sentenced in accord with law. To Crito's chagrin, Socrates rejects Crito's offer. Plato reports their conversation in his dialogue, *Crito*.

Why would Socrates pass up an opportunity to save his life? Plato, in his dialogue, *Crito*, reports Socrates's explanation.

* After Crito tells Socrates that if he refuses to escape, many people will assume that Crito was afraid to help him, Socrates replies that we shouldn't worry about what "the many" think. (2) "Good men," he says, "...(who) are the only persons worth considering, will think of these things truly as they occurred." (3) Further, Socrates says, "the many" who will mock me for dying don't understand that "not life, but a good life, is to be chiefly valued." (4)

* To defy the order of the court, Socrates says, would be to answer one wrong with another. This is never justified because:

"...(W)e must do no wrong."
"...(W)hen injured," we should never "injure in return."
"...(W)e must injure no one at all."
"...(W)e ought not to retaliate or render evil for evil to any one, whatever evil we may have suffered from him."
"...(N)either injury, nor retaliation nor warding off evil by evil is ever right." (5)

* If citizens opt to defy the law whenever they want to, then eventually government will collapse. In an imaginary dialogue between the government and Socrates, the government says to Socrates:

"...(A)re you not going by an act of yours to overturn us – the laws and the whole state as far as in you lies? Do you imagine that a state can subsist and not be overthrown, in which the decisions of law have no power, but are set aside and trampled upon by individuals?" (6)

* Government has provided me with a rich variety of benefits, ranging from education to protection. For this I should be grateful. Defying government now, Socrates implies, would make me an ingrate. (7)
* When I was young, Socrates points out, I chose to stay rather than leave after having had the opportunity to observe the government of Athens. By doing so, I entered into an *implied contract* with government in which I promised to obey it in exchange for all the benefits it affords citizens. By escaping I would break that promise. (8)
* Under this implied contract, Socrates continues, if I object to a law, I must gently entreat government to modify it. I have made no entreaty and I have been effusive in my praise of my government. I would be a hypocrite if I run now. (9)
* At my trial I proclaimed that I "preferred death to exile." It is too late now to change my mind. The law must run its course. (10)

Thus, through Socrates, Plato argues that a citizen has an absolute duty to obey government. There are no conditions that could arise - even saving one's own life - which would excuse a citizen from her duty to comply. If a citizen finds a law objectionable, she must respectfully petition government to change it. Meanwhile, she must comply. (We'll evaluate Plato's arguments after we deal with Dr. King.) Further, Plato seems to say that government is the foundation of our rights and duties; government (not nature or a social contract or God) confers rights and duties upon the citizens. As we'll see later in this chapter, Plato explicitly argues this position in *The Republic*.

Dr. Martin Luther King, Jr.

A Baptist minister with a church in Atlanta, Dr. Martin Luther King, Jr., became a reluctant leader in the struggle against racial discrimination in education, housing, employment, voting, transportation, restaurants, and lodging throughout the south. In 1963, Birmingham, Alabama, became his focus. Efforts by local black leaders to negotiate concessions with City Hall and local business owners had failed. (11) King, head of the Southern Christian Leadership Conference, joined with Rev. Fred Shuttlesworth of the Alabama Christian Movement for Human Rights, and hundreds of others in a series of non-violent sit-ins and marches that led to King's arrest. (12) During his eight-day incarceration, he was brought a statement signed by seven local Christian ministers and a rabbi attacking his activities as "unwise and untimely" and urging him and other "outsiders" to leave so that local leaders could solve local problems. He decided to craft a response which became known as the *Letter from Birmingham Jail.*

In response to the claim that the demonstrations were unwise and untimely, Dr. King observes that "Negroes" have waited "three hundred and forty years for our constitutional and God given-rights," (13) and that "freedom is never voluntarily given by the oppressor; it must be demanded by the oppressed." (14) He also accuses his critics of falling victim to the "myth of time," the assumption that "there is something in the very flow of time that will inevitably cure all ills." He answers that "time is neutral." "Human progress never tolls in on wheels of inevitability. It comes through the tireless efforts and persistent work" of courageous human beings. (15) In response to the claim that he was an outsider, Dr. King points out in the *Letter* that he was invited to Birmingham by local blacks after repeated attempts to win concessions had failed and that injustice in any part of the United States is a legitimate concern of all Americans. (16)

In that the protests in Birmingham were illegal – they were held without a parade permit which City Hall refused to grant – Dr. King gives a justification of the violation of law by protestors. He notes that there are two types of laws – just and unjust. "A just law," he says, "is a man-made code that squares with the moral law, or the law of God. An unjust law is a code that is out of harmony with the moral law." He quotes St. Augustine to the effect that "an unjust law is no law at all." (17) All segregation statutes, he argues, are unjust because they degrade human beings.

Dr. King made it clear in the *Letter* that non-violent protestors are not criminals. He contrasted *criminal* disobedience and *civil* disobedience. Criminals break just laws for personal gain, they strive to avoid punishment, they prefer secrecy, and they often use violence. By contrast, civil resisters break unjust laws to improve the community, they are willing to be punished, they welcome publicity, and they repudiate violence. In a key passage, he writes:

I hope you are able to see the distinction I am trying to point out. In no sense do I advocate evading or defying the law, as would the rabid segregationist. That would lead to anarchy. One who breaks an unjust law must do so openly, lovingly, and with a willingness to accept the penalty. I submit that an individual who breaks a law that conscience tells him is unjust, and who willingly accepts the penalty of imprisonment in order to arouse the conscience of the community over its injustice, is in reality expressing the highest respect for the law. (18)

Dr. King had learned much about non-violence from Mohandas Gandhi (1869-1948), leader of the independence movement in India before and during World War II. (Both Gandhi and Dr. King were influenced by Henry David Thoreau's *On the Duty of Civil Disobedience*.) Gandhi proposed non-violent resistance, which he called *satyagraha*, soul-force or truth-force, as far superior to violence in solving problems and reconciling adversaries. Gandhi led hundreds of non-violent protests against British control of India in which tens of thousands of protestors were arrested. In essence, Dr. King brought *satyagraha* to the United States and applied it brilliantly. Dr. King and his leadership team held workshops on non-violence before all of their protests to cultivate "self-purification," a readiness to accept verbal and physical attacks without retaliation. Those who didn't have the self-discipline and courage to do this were turned away. (19)

Let's reflect on the *Crito* and the *Letter*. To reiterate, Plato and Dr. King agree on three important points: government is necessary, citizens should not use violence to change a law to which they object, and citizens have a duty to obey the law. They differ, however, on the nature of this duty; for Plato, the duty is unconditional; for Dr. King, it is conditional.

According to Dr. King, the moral law takes precedence over the civil law. If you believe that a civil law violates the moral law, then you may violate the objectionable law and press non-violently for change. Dr. King is convinced that a reasonably stable government can tolerate selective, morally motivated non-compliance with the law without great risk. Plato, on the other hand, objects on two grounds. Firstly, Plato challenges the distinction between the civil law and the moral law. For Plato, in *The Republic*, as we'll see in detail soon, the civil law in society should be enacted by leaders who grasp the Good, the highest of the Forms, so that the civil law is an embodiment of the moral law. Secondly, Plato sees non-compliance with the law for any reason as a prescription for disaster. Giving the go-ahead to citizens to defy a law to which they object for any reason undermines respect for the law and risks the collapse of government.

On the risks of non-compliance, history seems to support Dr. King. For example, the Government of the United States has survived not only crime but also protests - some legal, some not - against slavery, the subordination of women, child labor, sexual harassment, racial discrimination, and the proliferation of guns and rifles, among others. Indeed, these protests prompted desirable changes in some cases - what many would call *moral progress* - in law and custom.

On the other hand, Plato's concern about defiance of law should not be dismissed lightly. When citizens feel free to pick and choose the laws that they will obey, respect for the law deteriorates and, predictably, violations become common. Consider speed limits. Most drivers - 75% - exceed them. (20) As a result, tens of thousands of avoidable accidents occur every year. As speeding and other traffic infractions spread, road custom trumps road law, to the detriment of public safety.

The Modern Models of Government

In this section we will examine the three major types of government which we find in today's world – dictatorship, democracy, and communism.

Dictatorship

Dictatorship is government in which authority rests in the hands of a single individual or a handful of them. Most actual dictatorships draw their inspiration from Plato's *The Republic*, his outline of an ideal society, published around 380 BCE, and the *Leviathan* of Thomas Hobbes (1588-1679), published in 1651. Let's summarize these two influential books.

Plato

In *The Republic* Plato orchestrates a lengthy conversation among Socrates and a group of friends in which they address a variety of topics, including justice. As the conversation unfolds, justice is defined for society and the individual. Justice in society is *harmony among the three classes* – leaders, soldiers, and workers; justice in the individual is *harmony among the three parts of the soul* – reason, emotion, and appetite.

Justice in society is achieved when each of the classes performs its appointed function well. The leaders govern, the soldiers protect, and the workers produce.

A citizen will be placed in the class for which she is suited. Those with superior powers of reason will become leaders, those with courage will become soldiers (and perhaps, later, leaders) and the rest will become workers. Leaders are a tiny fraction of the population with access to two levels of reality. The first is a higher level, the *abstract or spiritual* one, a genuine and stable *reality*, which reason discloses to them. This level includes the *Forms* or *Essences*, the highest of which is the *Form of Good*. The second is a lower level, the *physical* one, a level of *appearance* and flux, which the senses disclose to them. Since they and only they possess knowledge, they and only they deserve to rule. (They are "philosopher-kings.") By contrast, workers, who are ignorant of the Forms and who grasp only the inferior reality of matter, are unfit for leadership (or any other role in government, including voting). Further, each class has a unique set of rights and duties which grow out of the function of the class. For instance, leaders are entitled to possess power but they must live an ascetic life of public service. (No private property, no marriage!) Soldiers are entitled to possess weapons and to indulge their sexual appetites but they may not own property and they must fight to the death, if necessary. Also, a soldier-parent will never know his or her offspring; all children will be raised by the State. Workers are entitled to accumulate property and to indulge their desires for food and sex but they may not reproduce or have any say-so about government. To foster acceptance of their status in society, the young will be advised by teachers that they have been formed from gold (leaders), silver (soldiers), or bronze (workers).

Plato sees a correspondence between the structure of society and the structure of the individual soul. Just as society has three classes – leaders, soldiers, and workers – so the soul has three parts – reason, emotion, and appetite. Just as a just society has harmony among the classes, with the leaders governing obedient soldiers and workers, so a person has harmony in the soul, with reason in command of emotion and appetite.

One of Plato's proposals had to shock his contemporaries: women are to occupy all three classes, depending on each woman's natural aptitude.

Finally, how does Plato view democracy? For him, given the inborn limitations of the workers - the great bulk of the population - government of, by, and for the people simply won't work.

Plato states the core of his ideal state as follows:

Until philosophers are kings, or the kings and princes of this world have the spirit and power of philosophy, and political greatness and wisdom meet in in one, and those commoner natures who pursue either to the exclusion of the other are compelled to stand aside, cities will never have rest from their evils, - no, nor the human race, as I believe, - and then only will this our State have a possibility of life and behold the light of day. (21)

Hobbes

Thomas Hobbes lived through arguably the most tumultuous period in British history prior to World War II. The Thirty Years War (1618-1648) pitted Protestants against Catholics across Europe. The British Civil War (1642-1651) pitted supporters of the monarchy against supporters of Parliament. Amid the violence, Hobbes turned to the science of his era, especially Galileo and Harvey, to help him understand if it is possible to achieve and maintain order. He concluded that the prospect of order depends on the recognition of a fact of human nature: *human beings are pleasure-seeking, pain-avoiding machines.* We do whatever promises us pleasure and we avoid whatever promises us pain, even if the pursuit of pleasure or the avoidance of pain requires us to harm others. Thus, our "natural" condition (i.e., the state of nature, society without government) is one of deadly conflict, *a state of war*, where "there is continual fear and danger of violent death, and the life of man is solitary, poor, nasty, brutish, and short." (22) This, he says, is a…

> …war of everyone against every one, where everyone is governed by his own reason, and he can make use of anything that may be a help to him in preserving his life against his enemies. It follows that in such a condition, every man has a right to everything, even to one another's body. (23)

Hobbes sees only one escape from this state of war. All humans must enter into a contract in which they agree to confer all their "power and strength upon one man, or upon (an) assembly of men" and obey the commands of this "mortal god" as though their own. (24) This sovereign is a "great Leviathan" whose terrifying power will establish order and preserve lives. How? By threatening the citizens with injury or death if they dare to defy the law. (25) Thus, order springs from fear! A corollary is that any effort to dilute the power of the sovereign, as in democracy, limited government, and the division of powers, is misguided, dangerous, and likely catastrophic. (26)

Plato builds his proposal of an ideal society on two related foundations: a theory of human nature and a theory of knowledge. He elevates a handful of the

philosophically trained to absolute authority on the pretext that reason is dominant in their souls and they possess superior rational powers which gives them
access to the higher world of the Forms. He relegates the great bulk of the population to political impotence on the pretext that appetite is dominant in their souls
and they possess inferior rational powers which restricts their knowledge to the
lower world of matter. Plato also apportions rights and duties by social class. If
Plato's theory of human nature or his theory of knowledge or both are flawed, as
I believe they are, then his plan for a stratified society led by philosopher-kings is
also flawed. While *personal virtue* – harmony in one's soul in Plato's terminology
- and *superior intelligence* are desirable in public officials, they are no guarantee
of effective leadership. Consider presidents of the United States. President Jimmy
Carter scored high on both counts but few presidential historians evaluate his
performance in the White House as outstanding. President Harry Truman scored
high on the former but not on the latter while President Bill Clinton scored high
on the latter but not on the former, yet historians rate both very favorably as
presidents. (27)

Moreover, Plato is guilty of naivete in imagining that rulers who wield absolute
power can be models of selfless dedication to duty. History - ancient, medieval,
modern, and contemporary - is replete with examples of abuse of authority and
self-serving by the powerful. As Lord Acton (1834-1902) wisely observed, "Power
tends to corrupt and absolute power corrupts absolutely."

As for Hobbes, his case for absolute government rests on a conception of
human nature that deserves scrutiny. For Hobbes, human beings are pleasure-
seeking, pain-avoiding machines who will murder, maim, rape, or steal whenever
there is an advantage in doing so, resulting in a natural condition of war. If Plato
naively sees *some* of us - the class of leaders - as angels, Hobbes cynically sees
all of us as devils. The only hope of self-preservation, Hobbes insists, is an absolute ruler who terrifies us into self-restraint. Perhaps Hobbes was a product of his
times, marked as they were by persisting religious and political strife. Nevertheless,
he overestimates the human capacity for evil and he underestimates the human
capacity for good. Further, living two centuries before Darwin, he had little if any
appreciation of the role of solidarity, compassion, and sacrifice in perpetuating
the species.

Finally, history speaks against both Plato and Hobbes on a key point. The
form of government which they said could not possibly work - democracy - has
been tried with impressive results in many nations. It turns out that the masses

are educable. It turns out that a society doesn't necessarily sink into chaos if the power of leaders is limited. It turns out that most people are not rapacious animals. It turns out that people from the working class can become knowledgeable and effective public servants. It turns out that liberty is compatible with order.

Democracy

We look next at democracy, a system of government in which power is limited and divided, and majority rule prevails. To help us, we enlist the aid of two architects of this system – John Locke (1632-1704) and John Stuart Mill (1806-1873). We will focus on Locke's *The Second Treatise of Government* and Mill's *On Liberty*.

Locke

In *The Second Treatise of Government*, Locke sets forth his theory as to why and how we form government, how we should structure it, and what we may do if it fails. To do this, Locke says, we need to retreat to a stage of history before government, what he calls the "state of nature." (28) In the state of nature, we are free to live as we wish as long as we obey the *law of nature*. This is the moral law which reason discloses to us. (29) It teaches us that:

> Every one, as he is bound to preserve himself and not to quit his station willfully, so by the like reason, when his own preservation comes not in competition, ought he, as much as he can, to preserve the rest of mankind, and may not, unless it be to do justice to an offender, take away or impair the life, or what tends to the preservation of the life, the liberty, health, limb, or goods of another. (30)

In other words, Locke holds that the moral law confers upon human beings *rights* (or entitlements) to life, liberty, and estate (possessions). (31) He refers to these rights collectively as *property*, from the Latin term *proprius* which mean's one's own. The moral law also confers upon humans the authority to protect their rights. He calls this *the executive power of the law of nature*. (32) Under this authority a person may restrain, punish, and take reparation from a wrongdoer. (33) Punishment, Locke says, should be proportioned to the severity of the offense and aimed to *deter* the wrongdoer and others from future violations of rights. (34)

Locke devotes an entire chapter – *Chapter VI: Of Paternal Power* - in the *Second Treatise* to a discussion of the relation of parents to their children. He argues three points of importance:

- Paternal authority should be called *parental* authority because mother and father share it co-equally. (35)
- Parents are a child's *guardians*. It is their responsibility to raise, nourish, and educate the child until it is an adult, at which point their authority ceases. (36)
- Grown children owe their parents respect and support commensurate with the quality of the parents' role as guardians. (37)

So, what happens in the *society without government - a state of nature -* that spurs a transition to a *society with government – civil or political society*? According to Locke, life in the state of nature causes problems so severe that, out of desperation, people look to government for a solution. There are three main problems:

1. Many people do not follow the law of nature due to ignorance or malice. As a result, crime is rampant. Rights are constantly in jeopardy to a point that survival hangs in the balance.
2. When there are alleged violations of rights, there is no "known and indifferent judge" because people show bias in their own cases.
3. Many criminals go unpunished because victims lack the power to apprehend and punish them. (38)

So, in effect, society without government is a hell on earth. Accordingly, people enter into a social contract wherein they agree to **leave the state of nature forever, turn over to society the executive power of the law of nature, adopt majority rule (*lex majoris partis*), and establish government.** The purpose of government is to protect the *property* of the people, that is, their rights to life, liberty, and estate. People confer upon government the power to make laws (*legislative*), to administer and enforce laws (*executive*), and to conduct relations with other governments (*federative*). Locke specifies that the legislative power is conferred upon one segment of government and the executive and federative powers upon another. (This is his division of powers into what we call "branches" today.

For Locke there is no separate judiciary; judges are appointed by the executive power.) (39)

Finally, according to Locke, if government fails in its mission, as judged by the majority, the people are entitled to relief. After all, government, their "agent" or "deputy," is their creation and it is responsible to them. They may remove officials of government, alter the form of government, and, should those in power refuse to comply, opt for rebellion or revolution. For Locke, ultimately, "The people shall be judge..." (40)

Mill

A second important shaper of democracy is John Stuart Mill (1806-1883), a Utilitarian. We had a look at his moral theory in Chapter 5: Right and Wrong. From that, especially the Greatest Happiness Principle, one could get the impression that the individual takes a back seat to the group. But Mill's *On Liberty* (1859), published the same year as Darwin's *Origin of Species*, sends a very different message. *Liberties* for Mill are *rights* or *immunities*, spheres of behavior that are reserved to the individual and shielded from interference by government. (41) Clearly, Mill saw democracy as a huge improvement over authoritarian regimes, so common in history. Yet he detected a flaw in the theory and practice of democracy as he watched it evolve during the 19th century. The problem is a new threat to the individual - the *tyranny of the majority*. This is the tendency for "the most numerous or the most *active* part of the people" (42) to infringe upon the rights of the individual by *law* and by *custom*. (43)

To combat the tyranny of the majority and to resuscitate liberty, tolerance, and individuality, Mill proposes "one very simple principle":

That principle is that the sole end for which mankind are warranted, individually or collectively, in interfering with the liberty of action of any of their number is self-protection. That the only purpose for which power can be rightfully exercised over any member of a civilized community, against his will, is to prevent harm to others. His own good, either physical or moral, is not a sufficient warrant... The only part of the conduct of anyone for which he is amenable to society is that which concerns others. In the part which merely concerns himself, his independence is, of right, absolute. Over himself, over his own body and mind, the individual is sovereign. (44)

Mill makes three important points about this principle: it applies only to adults, not children (45), it recognizes that an individual can harm others through both *action* and *inaction* (46), and it is *useful* both to the individual and to society. (47)

Mill spends a significant part of *On Liberty* arguing the last point. He recognizes three "regions" of liberty: *consciousness, tastes and pursuits*, and *combination*. (48)

Liberty of consciousness means the right to shape and express one's own ideas on all subjects; liberty of tastes and pursuits means the right to adopt the life style that one wants; and liberty of combination means the right to associate with whom one wants for any purpose. (49) How are these liberties useful to self and others? Let's take liberty of consciousness. It is useful to you because it enables you to pursue the truth without censors looking over your shoulder; it makes you master of what you believe and say. But it is also useful to society. If a novel belief turns out to be true and the prevailing belief is false, we can learn truth for the first time. If, however, the novel belief turns out to be false and the prevailing belief is true, we can gain a "clearer perception and livelier impression of truth produced by its collision with error." (50) Thus, liberty of consciousness produces growth in knowledge. (51) As for liberty of tastes and pursuits, Mill argues that just as ideas need to be injected into the marketplace of ideas to enable us to sort good ideas from bad ones, so too, different life styles, "different experiments" in living, need to be tried out to enable us to learn which life style promotes our fulfillment and which does not. In ideas as in life styles, mindless conformity deprives both the individual and society of fresh paths to happiness. (52)

While it is difficult to exaggerate the influence of Locke and Mill, their political theories are not without problems. As for Locke, anthropologists tell us that few if any societies ever had a period without a sanctioned system of governance - whether or not we call it a government - in one form or another. The state of nature is more an imaginary condition than an actual one. Also, while Locke emphasizes that rights accrue to human beings as human beings, many people who lived during and after him in England and elsewhere - for instance, slaves, women, and non-owners of property - did not enjoy such rights. (I grant that it is a bit unfair to take issue with Locke on this, however. After all, his stand for limited government is a turning point in history, he did take a stand for women's rights in his doctrine of parental power, and slavery was so embedded in western culture that it persisted for over 160 years after his death.) Finally, Locke never fully appreciated the tension between the right to liberty and the principle of majority rule. Happily, Mill did. Indeed, his *On Liberty* is largely a paean to liberty and an indictment of majority excess. On the other hand, Mill's criterion of harm is vague; in many cases, harm is in the eye of the beholder. Take atheism, for instance. Locke saw atheists as so harmful to society that he denied them toleration. Locke's suspicions are widely shared even today in the United States. Finally, Mill's concern about the tyranny of the majority reached a point that his commitment to democracy was suspect. In *Thoughts on Parliamentary Reform* (1859), for instance, he argued against the secret ballot and called for "plural voting" whereby the votes of the educated would carry more weight than those of the uneducated. Another work, *Considerations on Representative Government* (1861), is downright elitist in parts. (53)

Communism

The third modern model of government is communism. To understand this, let us turn to its principal shaper, Karl Marx (1818-1883), and his collaborator, Friedrich Engels (1820-1895).

Marx and Engels

Did Locke and Mill ensure the triumph of democracy in the modern world? Would tyranny - of one or of many – succumb to Locke's majority rule and Mill's individuality? Would more and more citizens cast ballots and fewer and fewer face pressures to conform? Would self-government reign? To Marx and Engels, those who answer *yes* to these questions are naïve. They fail to understand that unless you change the economy, you change nothing; short of a transformation of the system of production and distribution, government of, by, and for the people is a dream. Almost 150 years before the phrase surfaced in U.S. politics in the 1990s, Marx and Engels proclaimed, in so many words, "It's the economy, stupid!"

Marx and Engels co-authored *The Manifesto of the Communist Party* which was published in 1848. In the *Preface* to the 1888 edition of the *Manifesto*, Engels states the central insight of the *Manifesto*:

...(T)he fundamental proposition which forms its nucleus belongs to Marx. That proposition is: That in every historical epoch the prevailing mode of economic production and exchange, and the social organization necessarily following from it, form the basis upon which is built up, and from which alone can be explained, the political and intellectual history of that epoch; that, consequently, the whole history of mankind (since the dissolution of primitive tribal society, holding land in common ownership) has been a history of class struggles, contests between exploiting and exploited, ruling and oppressed classes; that the history of these class struggles forms a series of evolutions in which, nowadays, a stage has been reached where the exploited and oppressed class - the proletariat - cannot attain its emancipation from the sway of the exploiting and ruling class - the bourgeoisie - without at the same time, and once for all, emancipating society at large from all exploitation, oppression, class distinctions and class struggles. (54)

According to Marx and Engels, every society develops a system to produce the goods and services which it needs. In each system there are a variety of roles, some wielding more influence than others. Those who perform the same or similar roles in the scheme of production and exchange occupy the same social *class*. Every society therefore has a variety of classes:

In ancient Rome we have patricians, knights, plebeians, slaves; in the Middle Ages, feudal lords, vassals, guild masters, journeymen, apprentices, serfs; in almost all of these classes, again, subordinate gradations. The modern bourgeois that has sprouted from the ruins of feudal society has not done away with class antagonisms. It has but established new classes, new conditions of oppression, new forms of struggle in place of the old ones. (55)

There is a continuing tension among these classes – subtle and peaceful at some times, obvious and violent at others. Individuals in a lower class naturally seek to move to a higher one and all classes naturally seek to *maintain or enhance* their power, influence, and status vis-à-vis other classes. Once the existing economy cannot contain the class conflict, there is a revolution, usually bloody, which brings a new chapter in history replete with a new economic scheme and a new array of classes. The drama of history, as Marx and Engels describe it, bears a similarity to the state of nature of Hobbes and Locke with two important exceptions – *the conflict is principally among classes, not individuals, and government in some form exists, but it is either weak or it is a tool of the dominant class or both.*

So, for Marx and Engels, the prospect of rights, majority rule, and autonomy is negligible as long as economic and political arrangements perpetuate control by the few. Alas, the picture looks quite bleak. Is there any hope? Yes, indeed, they insist! Marx and Engels were convinced that a new and promising stage in history was reached during their own era which would eventually sound the death knell for oppression and class struggle:

> Our epoch, the epoch of the bourgeoisie, possesses, however, this distinctive feature: it has simplified the class antagonisms. Society as a whole is more and more splitting up into two great hostile camps, into two great classes directly facing each other: Bourgeoisie and Proletariat. (56)

The bourgeoisie consists of owners - *capitalists* - who own the productive apparatus of society (land, forests, factories, machines, mines, minerals, ships, etc.), who employ workers for wages in the quest for profit, who own mansions at home and abroad, who attend the finest private schools and colleges, who have access to state-of-the-art medical care, and who use their wealth to control government. The proletariat consists of workers - young and old - who sell their labor to the bourgeoisie for wages, who struggle to survive in the slums of cities, who have no formal education, who have no medical care, whose jobs disappear sooner or later due to automation, and who are politically impotent.

Marx and Engels tell us that, as capitalism matures, the bourgeoisie unavoidably invite their own destruction and usher in the ascendancy of the proletariat. They compete with one another for efficiencies in production, for workers, and for foreign markets. The big fish swallow the small ones. Wealth becomes concentrated more and more and the losers sink into the expanding proletariat. The bourgeoisie attract huge numbers of workers from the countryside to the city where they live, work, and suffer side by side, sowing the seeds of class consciousness. With a world market, national businesses give way to international ones. As growing numbers of workers lose their jobs or suffer wage decreases, the pool of consumers shrinks and there is overproduction. As workers suffer more and more, solidarity intensifies. Workers overcome barriers of distance, race, language, religion, and ethnicity. Nation by nation, they form unions, get involved in politics, and demand change. (57) Eventually, a civil war erupts in which they overthrow the bourgeoisie and institute far-reaching change. (58) With the aid of intellectuals, who throw in with them (59), the proletariat gain control of the government and the economy, abolish private property, centralize the process of production and distribution, and embark on an ambitious overhaul of society to provide housing, education, medical care, food, clothes, leisure, and the arts for everyone. (60)

In time we have communism - *a mix of democracy and socialism*, classes no longer exist, social harmony prevails (61), political equality is a reality, work is fulfilling and varied (62), and self-government is possible for the first time.

Let's focus, finally, on Marx's assessment of religion in a capitalist society. In his *Critique of Hegel's Philosophy of Right*, he writes:

> Religious suffering is at the same time the expression of real suffering and the protest against real suffering. Religion is the sigh of the oppressed creature, the sentiment of a heartless world, and the soul of soulless conditions. It is the opium of the people. The abolition of religion as the illusory happiness of the people is the demand for their real happiness. (63)

Thus, Marx holds that religion in capitalism functions as a drug which sedates the working class, making it docile. It does this by proclaiming that life on earth is a temporary journey, filled with suffering, which gives way to our real and permanent destination, heaven, where we will enjoy unbounded happiness in the presence of God. For Marx, this seduction defuses potential working class anger and hostility toward the bourgeoisie and preserves the status quo, at least for a time. He anticipates that religion will disappear in the enlightened post-capitalist society of communism. Marx would have been shocked to find religious voices in a capitalist society that demanded social justice in the here and now in the form of generous wages; safety in the workplace; limits on work hours; free, universal public education; access to medical care and decent housing; and so on. Any minister, priest, rabbi, or imam with this message, Marx no doubt expected, would be subject to arrest, prosecution, and, in all likelihood, death.

Let's evaluate now what Marx and Engels had to say. On the plus side, they made important contributions to political theory and practice. They drew attention to the reality of classes; they highlighted (and probably inflated) the impact of the economy; they warned that government, even a "democracy," can be an agent of the few who are wealthy and their acolytes instead of the many who are not (64); they warned that prevailing patterns of thought and action can impede progress; they accurately predicted many of the positive and negative developments in capitalism; they pointed out the social costs of an unregulated market; and they inspired millions to work for change. Nevertheless, their plan to rescue the workers of the world and establish genuine democracy was ill-conceived. In nations which proclaimed communism, the post-revolutionary period, the dictatorship of the proletariat, turned out to be a nightmare. The sympathetic intellectuals, the "vanguard of the proletariat," who were supposed to serve as guides and helpers, wield power temporarily, upgrade the standard of living, and prepare the ground for full-scale democracy failed on all counts. The Communist Party elite became a surrogate bourgeoisie. Corruption was rampant. Dissent was punished. Religion was driven underground. Resources were diverted from the reconstruction of society to armaments and defense. The government-controlled media censored the news - local, national, and international - and rationalized failures to meet production goals. Improvements in the standard of living were meager. Eventually, as in the USSR, the system collapsed of its own weight. The road to communism turned out to be a dead end.

Footnotes:

1. From *Summa Theologica* in *The Basic Writings of Saint Thomas Aquinas*, Volume Two, Question 90, Article 4, Edited and Annotated, with an Introduction, by Anton C. Pegis, Random House, 1945, p. 747.
2. Plato, *Crito*, in *The Dialogues of Plato*, Volume One, Translated by Benjamin Jowett, Random House, 1937, p. 428.
3. *Ibid.*, p. 428.
4. *Ibid.*, p. 432.
5. *Ibid.*, p. 433. Note the similarity to the Sermon of the Mount. See especially Matthew 5, verses 38-48. Jesus counsels us to reject "an eye for an eye" and to love everyone, even our enemies.
6. *Ibid.*, p. 434.
7. *Ibid.*, pp. 434-435.
8. *Ibid.*, pp. 435-436.
9. *Ibid.*, p. 436.
10. *Ibid.*, p. 436.
11. The Governor of Alabama, George Wallace, ran on a platform of 'segregation forever." The Mayor of Birmingham was a segregationist, as was Chief of Police Eugene "Bull" Conner, who turned police dogs on non-violent protestors in full view of a national TV audience. Seventeen black churches and houses in Birmingham were bombed from 1957 to 1962. Of the 80,000 registered voters in Birmingham, only 10,000 were blacks, despite the fact that 40% of the city population was black. See "Birmingham," sparknotes.com.
12. Dr. King and his associates were arrested for assembling without a parade permit. They had been denied one when they applied for one at the Birmingham City Hall. King says in the *Letter* that the ordinance requiring a permit is fine in principle but objectionable when it is exploited

to impede the exercise of the rights to peaceful assembly and peaceful protest afforded by the Constitution.

13. Dr. Martin Luther King, Jr., *Letter from Birmingham Jail*, in *Why We Can't Wait*, Beacon Press, 2010, p. p. 91.

14. *Ibid.*, p. 91.

15. *Ibid.*, p. 98.

16. *Ibid.*, p. 87.

17. *Ibid.*, p. 93.

18. *Ibid.*, pp. 94-95.

19. In the *Letter* Dr. King points out that the strategy of non-violence encompasses four successive stages: "collection of the facts to determine whether injustices are alive, negotiation, self-purification, and direct action." The *Letter*, p. 87.

20. Source: The National Highway Traffic Safety Administration. See www. trafficviolationlawfirms. com. The NHTSA also reports the following: 80% of younger drivers exceed the speed limit; 40% of drivers run red lights; 30% of drivers make "rolling stops"; 25% of drivers don't use seat belts; 17% of drivers pass on the shoulder in heavy traffic; 12% of drivers make angry, insulting, or obscene gestures to other drivers; and 10% of drivers cut in front of oncoming cars. Weaving and tailgating are also quite common. 60% of those who died in traffic accidents in a recent year did not wear seat belts. Although the percentage of impaired drivers has dropped from 7.5% to 2.5% over the past thirty years, 1.4 million tickets were issued in 2006 to impaired drivers.

21. See Plato, *The Republic*, Book V, in *The Dialogues of Plato*, Translated by Benjamin Jowett, Volume One, Random House, 1937, p. 737.

22. Thomas Hobbes, *Leviathan*, Edited by Marshall Missner, Pearson Longman, 2008, p. 83.

23. *Ibid.*, pp. 86-87.

24. *Ibid.*, p. 116.

25. *Ibid.*, p. 116. A leviathan is a sea monster mentioned in the Old Testament.

26. Hobbes supported an absolute monarchy in England.

27. Siena College conducts a survey periodically in which presidential historians rank the U.S. presidents. Jimmy Carter is ranked #32, Harry Truman #9, and Bill Clinton #13 among the 43 presidents.

28. John Locke, *The Second Treatise of Government*, The Library of Liberal Arts, 1952, p. 4.

29. *Ibid.*, p. 5.

30. *Ibid.*, p. 6.

31. For Locke, estate refers to one's possessions (for instance, land, a house, a barn, animals, clothes, a wagon, etc.). One acquires estate, according to Locke, through one's labor. One's labor transforms what was common to what is private. (pp. 16-17) Locke sets limits to accumulation,

however. One must leave for others as much and as good as one takes, and one may not take so much that it spoils. (pp. 17-19) The agreement to introduce money, however, results in levels of wealth since money doesn't spoil. (p. 22, p. 28.) This is also true of gold and silver. (p. 29)

32. Locke, *The Second Treatise...*, pp. 6-7, p. 9.

33. *Ibid.*, pp. 6-7. A person who threatens the rights of another person, according to Locke, renounces reason, which is the standard appropriate to humans, and opts instead for force, which is the standard appropriate to animals. One who opts for force forfeits her rights under the moral law and authorizes others to destroy her, if necessary, as "a wild savage beast." (p. 8) Through the use of force or the intention to use it, a wrongdoer, Locke says, declares a "state of war" upon the victim. (p. 11) Also, see pp. 12-13.

34. *Ibid.*, pp. 6-7.

35. *Ibid.*, p. 30.

36. *Ibid.*, pp. 33-34.

37. *Ibid.*, p. 38.

38. *Ibid.*, p. 71.

39. *Ibid.*, Chapters VII to XII, pp. 44-84.

40. The discussion of the options of the governed if and when their government fails occurs mainly in Chapter XIX, *Of the Dissolution of Government*, pp. 119-139. The quote is from p. 138.

41. John Stuart Mill, *On Liberty*, The Library of Liberal Arts, Inc., 1956, p. 4.

42. *Ibid.*, p. 6.

43. *Ibid.*, p. 7. According to Mill, religion produces the most common expression of the tyranny of the majority in the modern world. When it comes to religion, the majority typically demands uniformity and suppresses dissent. As a result, "...religious freedom has hardly anywhere been practically realized..." and "...even in the most tolerant countries, the duty of toleration is admitted with tacit reserves..." Mill, *On Liberty*, p. 11.

44. *Ibid.*, p. 13. A few pages later, Mill clarifies the phrase "merely concerns himself." He says that it means "directly and in the first instance" and he concedes that "whatever affects himself may affect others through himself..."
(p. 16) For Mill, then, if your actions affect others but threaten no harm to them, society has no justification for interference.

45. *Ibid.*, p. 13. Apparently, these intellectuals bolt from the class of bourgeoisie.

46. *Ibid.*, p. 15. Examples of harming others through inaction which Mill gives are an individual refusing to testify in court and to "share in the common defense." (p. 15)

47. *Ibid.*, p. 14, p. 16.

48. *Ibid.*, p. 16.

49. *Ibid.*, p. 16.

50. *Ibid.*, p. 21, p. 64. Mill points out that the most common situation in a conflict between a novel and a prevailing belief is when both have a measure of truth and of falsity. (p. 57)

51. Mill adds that an indispensable condition of our justified confidence in a belief is that it remains open to challenge. (p. 24) He notes: "Both teachers and learners go to sleep at their post as soon as there is no enemy in the field." (p. 52)

52. Mill justifies the utility of the liberty of tastes and pursuits and, to a lesser extent, the liberty of combination, in Chapter III, *Of Individuality, as One of the Elements of Well-Being*, pp. 67-90.

53. Professor Curran Shields, Editor of the edition of *On Liberty* cited above, charges that in this work Mill repudiates "the distinctive principles of democratic rule." Editor's Introduction, *On Liberty*, p. xiv.

54. Friedrich Engels, *Preface* to the 1888 edition of *The Manifesto of the Communist Party*, in *Great Books of the Western World*, Volume 50, 1952, p. 416. Engels opines that this proposition is as important to understanding history as Darwin's to understanding biology. (p. 416)

55. Marx and Engels, *The Manifesto*, in *Karl Marx: The Essential Writings*, edited by Frederic L. Bender, Westview Press, 1986, p. 241.

56. *Ibid.*, pp. 241-242.

57. According to *The Manifesto*, "Though not in substance, yet in form, the struggle of the proletariat with the bourgeoisie is at first a national struggle. The proletariat of each country must, of course, first of all settle matters with its own bourgeoisie." (p. 252)

58. *Ibid.*, p. 252.

59. *Ibid.*, p. 251.

60. *Ibid.*, pp. 261-263.

61. Marx writes: "It (communism) is the definitive resolution of the antagonism between man and nature, and between man and man. It is the true solution of the conflict between existence and essence, between objectification and self-affirmation, between freedom and necessity, between individual and species." Karl Marx, *Early Writings*, McGraw-Hill, 1964, p. 155.

62. Friedrich Engels notes that: "In communist society, where nobody has one exclusive sphere of activity but (where) each has become accomplished in any branch he wishes, society regulates the general production and thus makes it possible for me to do one thing today and another tomorrow, to hunt in the morning, fish in the afternoon, rear cattle in the evening, criticize after dinner, just as I have a mind, without ever becoming hunter, fisherman, shepherd or critic." Friedrich Engels, *German Ideology*, International Publishers, 1960, p. 22.

63. Karl Marx, *Introduction to A Contribution to the Critique of Hegel's Philosophy of Right*, Collected Works, Volume 3, 1976. Also see, *Essential Writings of Karl Marx*, Edited with an Introduction and Notes by David Caute, Collier Books, 1967, p. 87.

64. C. Wright Mills exposed this about U.S. democracy in his classic, *The Power Elite*, Oxford University Press, 1956.

Recommendations for Further Study:

1. Thomas Aquinas, *Summa Theologica, XIII. Law*, Questions 90-108, many editions.
2. Plato, *Crito*, and *The Republic*, many editions.
3. Martin Luther King, Jr., *Why We Can't Wait*, Beacon Press, 2010.
4. Thomas Hobbes, *Leviathan*, many editions.
5. Richard Peters, *Hobbes*, Peregrine Books, 1967.
6. John Locke, *The First Treatise of Government*, *The Second Treatise of Government*, and *Letter Concerning Toleration*, many editions.
7. Alexander Hamilton, James Madison, and John Jay, *The Federalist*, 1787-1788, many editions.
8. Jason BeDuhn, "Why the Supreme Court's *Hobby Lobby* Ruling is Even Worse Than You Think," *Church & State*, October 2014, pp. 19-20.
9. John Stuart Mill, *On Liberty*, many editions.
10. John Stuart Mill, *The Subjection of Women*, many editions.
11. John Rawls, *A Theory of Justice*, Harvard University Press, 1971.
12. *Reading Rawls: Critical Studies of A Theory of Justice*, edited by Norman Daniels, Basic Books, n.d.
13. Robert Nozick, *Anarchy, State, and Utopia*, Basic Books, 1974.
14. *Karx Marx: The Essential Writings*, edited by Frederick L. Bender, Westview Press, 1986.
15. Ayn Rand, *Capitalism: The Unknown Ideal*, Signet Books, 1967.
16. John Dewey, *The Public and Its Problems*, The Swallow Press, n.d.
17. John Dewey, *Democracy and Education*, Free Press, 1967.
18. C. Wright Mills, *The Power Elite*, Oxford University Press, 1956.
19. C. Wright Mills, *The Sociological Imagination*, Oxford University Press, 1969.
20. *The New Sociology: Essays in Social Science and Social Theory in Honor of C. Wright Mills*, edited by Irving Louis Horowitz, Oxford University Press, 1965.
21. David Kelley, *A Life of One's Own: Individual Rights and the Welfare State*, Cato Institute, 1998.
22. Thomas Shipka, *Social Conflict and Reconstruction*, University Microfilms, Doctoral Dissertation, Boston College, 1969.
23. Sidney Hook, *Marx and the Marxists*, Van Nostrand Reinhold Company, 1955.
24. Sidney Hook, *Marxism and Beyond*, Rowman and Littlefield, 1983.
25. Sidney Hook, *The Hero in History*, Beacon Press, 1955.
26. *Women Without Superstition: No Gods – No Masters*, edited by Annie Laurie Gaylor, Freedom from Religion Foundation, 1997.
27. Erik H. Erikson, *Gandhi's Truth*, W. W. Norton & Co., Inc., 1969.
28. Richard A. Clarke, *Your Government Failed You*, HarperCollins, 2008.
29. David Kuo, *Tempting Faith*, Free Press, 2006.

30. Chris Hedges, *American Fascists*, Free Press, 2006.

31. James K. Galbraith, *The Predator State*, Free Press, 2008.

32. Carl Cohen, *Four Systems*, Random House, 1982.

33. Jimmy Carter, *Our Endangered Values*, Simon & Schuster, 2005.

34. Garry Wills, *Head and Heart: American Christianities*, The Penguin Press, 2007.

35. Juan Williams, *Muzzled: The Assault on Honest Debate*, Crown, 2011.

36. Carl Hart, *High Time*, Harper, 2013.

37. David L. Holmes, *The Faiths of the Founding Fathers*, Oxford University Press, 2006.

38. James O'Toole, "Natural Rights," pp. 174-206, *The Great Ideas Today: 1998*, Encyclopedia Britannica, Inc., 1998.

39. Susan Jacoby, *Freethinkers: A History of American Secularism*, Metropolitan Books, 2004; Holt Paperbacks, 2005.

40. Shadi Hamid, *Temptations of Power: Islamists & Illiberal Democracy in a New Middle East*, Oxford University Press, 2014.

41. Robert Boston, *Taking Liberties: Why Religious Freedom Doesn't Give You Power To Tell Other People What To Do*, Prometheus Books, 2014.

42. Shadia B. Drury, "Vanquishing Evil," *Free Inquiry*, December 2014/January 2015, pp. 13, 44-45.

43. Charles J. Sykes, *How the Right Lost Its Mind*, St. Martin's Press, 2017.

44. Jeff Flake, *Conscience of a Conservative*, Random House, 2017.

45. Douglas Murray, *The Strange Death of Europe: Immigration, Identity, Islam*, Bloomsbury, 2017.

46. Malcolm Nance, *The Plot to Hack America: How Putin's Cyberspies and WikiLeaks Tried to Steal the 2016 Election*, Second Edition, Skyhorse Publishing, 2017.

47. Michael Wolff, *Fire and Fury: Inside the Trump White House*, Henry Holt and Company, 2018.

Readings: Government

Is Socialism Coming?

Tom Shipka (2009)

In the United States today health care reform is front and center. President Obama has stumped for reform in dozens of appearances across the nation, an address to the Congress, and no fewer than five televised news shows last Sunday. On a daily basis the media report the latest wrinkles in a spate of health care proposals under discussion in the Congress and speculate on the political prospects of the President's preferred "public option."

In the health care debate, as in the government bailout of failing banks and two major U.S. auto producers, some critics of the White House invoke the "S" word – *socialism*. They warn that America is abandoning its historic commitment to limited government, private ownership, and the free market in favor of a welfare state, public ownership, and a planned economy. Such critics, including those attending TEA (Taxed Enough Already) parties, seem to share Ronald Reagan's distrust of government. Government, they believe, is the problem, not the solution. Government, they tell us, is inept, it covets more and more power, it steals from producers to support parasites, it threatens our liberties, and it saddles future generations with enormous debt. Setting aside the voices of dissent from the radical fringe - the birthers, the conspiracy theorists, those who vilify the President as a liar, and those who construe his pep talk to the nation's students as socialist propaganda - let's engage the central issue: Is the United States abandoning capitalism for socialism?

Let us understand that under socialism the government owns and administers the productive apparatus of society and provides all the goods and services, and by contrast, under capitalism individuals and companies own and administer the productive apparatus of society and provide all the goods and services with the possible exception of law enforcement and national defense. Now, where can we find examples of these two systems in practice? The fact is that we can't because the dominant economic system in the world today is a mixed one. A mixed economy incorporates elements of socialism and capitalism, although the mix differs from nation to nation. When a good or service is provided by a public source in a society, there is a socialist component; when a good or service is provided by a private source in a society, there is a capitalist component.

Thus, if you want to see socialist components in the United States, look no farther than the Grand Canyon National Park, Social Security, Head Start, Medicare, Medicaid, the U.S. Postal Service, food stamps (SNAP), police and fire departments, public schools, public colleges and universities, public libraries, and public parks. Similarly, if you want to see capitalist components in the United States, look no farther than Disney World, the stock market, McDonald's, Wal-Mart, Amazon, Microsoft, Omaha Steaks, UPS, ESPN, private schools, private colleges and universities, and banks and credit unions.

It seems clear to me that the U.S. is not abandoning capitalism for socialism. Rather, it continues to blend elements of both systems. Although the specific jurisdictions of the public and private sectors in America will change in the future as they have in the past, our economic hybrid is here to stay for the foreseeable future.

John Locke on the Separation of Church and State

Tom Shipka (2006)

The writings of John Locke, British philosopher who lived from 1632 to 1704, had such a powerful impact on the founders of the United States that it is not an exaggeration to speak about Locke as America's philosophical father.

One key writing of Locke which helped shaped the American experiment in limited government is his *Letter Concerning Toleration*. (1) This was published first in Latin in 1685, then later in English in 1689, and it addresses the issue of the proper relationship between church and state. Locke wrote the *Letter Concerning Toleration* because of his reservations about the Anglican church's extensive political power in England and his fears about "the ranting sectarianism of (various groups) of Dissenters, their dogmatic insistence that they alone held the key to salvation," and the likelihood of civil strife if they gained political ascendancy. (2)

In his *Letter Concerning Toleration* Locke lays down the framework for the principle of the separation of church and state. According to Locke, the state is a voluntary association of human beings whose purpose is to protect and promote their human rights and liberties while the church is a voluntary association of human beings whose purpose is to promote the salvation of their souls. The state passes and enforces laws and punishes lawbreakers as necessary by depriving them of their treasure or freedom or life. The church, by contrast, may not use coercion. Its only legitimate tools are "exhortations, admonitions, and advices." In other words, the state may use force but the church may use only arguments.

The key to understanding Locke lies in his insistence that religious beliefs are based on faith and that there is no way to demonstrate that one set of faith-based beliefs is true while another is false. Believers are entitled to embrace with devotion their own set of religious beliefs but they must respect and tolerate the right of others in or out of their own sect to disagree. Coercion may never be used by church or state to assure compliance with or dissent from any given religious belief system. Locke observed, "For every church is orthodox to itself, to others, erroneous or heretical." From this Locke concludes "And therefore peace, equity, and friendship are always mutually to be observed by particular churches, in the same manner as by private persons, without any pretense of superiority or jurisdiction over one another."

Locke laid down several rules of toleration.

* The state is required to tolerate churches as long as they tolerate one another and do nothing to jeopardize the human rights and liberties of citizens, including their own members.
* Since religious faith is voluntary and inward, neither a political nor an ecclesiastical authority may attempt to compel the individual citizen in matters of faith. If a church takes umbrage with one of its members, it may excommunicate him or her – period. And a church member may withdraw at any time from his or her congregation without penalty or prejudice.
* Further, no church may force or attempt to force its beliefs upon the state or upon society generally.
* No state may attempt to coerce citizens based on the religious beliefs of its leaders or of church groups in society. In all religious matters the individual must be guided by his or her conscience alone.
* Further, the leaders of government may not command that certain forms of worship be used or not used by the churches and the churches may not have practices which deny the civil rights of their members.
* Civil authorities may punish only civil offenses but not sins.
* Civil authorities may not impede the expression of opinions generally or in a particular church; and
* Civil authorities should not tolerate intolerant churches. All churches should "lay down toleration as the foundation of their own liberty, and teach that liberty of conscience is every man's natural right, equally belonging to dissenters as to themselves…"

Locke said that there are exceptions to the rule of toleration. For instance, churches teaching against civil interests, any church which insists on intolerance, atheists, and Papists, that is, Roman Catholics, are not to be tolerated. In the case of Catholics, Locke feared that they recognized the Pope as both an ecclesiastical and political sovereign. As for atheists, Locke believed that they lacked the foundation of morality which requires belief in God as an authoritative law-giver.

Although the United State of America eventually went beyond Locke in extending tolerance to Roman Catholics and atheists, Locke remains the architect of the principle of the separation of church and state in our nation.

I leave to your judgment whether our nation is faithful to the spirit and letter of Locke's famous treatise on toleration.

1.   John Locke, *A Letter Concerning Toleration*, in *John Locke on Politics and Education*, Edited by Howard R. Penniman, D. Van Nostrand Company, Inc., 1947, pp. 21-68. Quotations here are from this volume.

2.   *Ibid*, p. 17.

Religion and the Founders

Tom Shipka (2013)

In popular culture there are two sharply contrasting views about religion and the founding fathers. One is that the founders were devout Christians who read the Bible and prayed daily. The other is that they were products of the Enlightenment who abandoned religion for reason and science. So, which view is accurate? Neither! If we could take a snapshot of religion in the colonies in 1770, here is what we would find: (1)

- 1) The founders were born into a Christian culture. Nearly all of the 3,000,000 residents of the colonies were Christians, nine of the thirteen colonies had an official state church, and nine of the ten existing colleges were founded by religious groups to train their clergy and lay leaders;
- 2) Religious diversity was a fact of life. There were over twenty Christian sects in the colonies with strong differences on issues of faith; (2)
- 3) Religious toleration was more the exception than the rule. Rhode Island, founded by Roger Williams, and Pennsylvania, founded by William Penn, were the only colonies that welcomed all stripes of Christians and non-Christians; (3)
- 4) Deism, which originated in Europe, had infiltrated colonial culture among the educated class and challenged traditional religion. According to Deists:
  - * Reason, not faith, is the path to knowledge;
  - * The universe was designed by God, a Grand Architect, a First Cause who imbued it with natural laws and then retreated from it;
  - * If one wishes to know God, one must study God's complex handi-work, the universe;
  - * The Bible is a collection of myths and fables triggered by superstition;
  - * Jesus was an inspiring moral teacher but neither a god nor a savior; and
  - * Contrary to the teachings of Calvin, humans are neither depraved nor predestined;
- 5) Nearly all of the founders modified their Christian beliefs to a greater or lesser extent to accommodate Deism. As a result, the religious views of the

founders were scattered across a spectrum with traditional Christianity on one end and Deism on the other. The founders fell into three groups – *traditional Christians*, *Christian Deists*, and *Non-Christian Deists*. The majority were Christian Deists; (4) and

- 6) Despite their absorption of Deism, all of the founders but Benjamin Franklin attended their ancestral church at least occasionally, most of them never abandoned their ancestral church, and the wives and daughters of most of them remained traditional Christians.

Thus, the founders were religious hybrids and their religious views were complex and diverse. Commentators who paint a different picture, according to historian Robert Holmes, "revise history to align the founders' beliefs with their own." (5)

Given this broad range of religious views, it is all the more remarkable that the founders reached a consensus on key issues as the new nation emerged. They prized personal liberty; they opposed religious dogmatism, intolerance, and coercion; they valued civic virtue; they opposed compulsory support of churches; they sought to separate government from the churches; and they embraced the doctrines of natural rights, government by consent, limited government, the separation of powers, and majority rule. (6)

1. I rely here mainly on David L. Holmes, *The Faiths of the Founding Fathers*, Oxford University Press, 2006. Holmes is Walter G. Mason Professor of Religious Studies, Emeritus, at the College of William and Mary. Holmes spent 46 years at William and Mary. Among his other books are *A Brief History of the Episcopal Church* (1993) and *The Faiths of the Postwar Presidents: From Truman to Obama* (2012). *The Faiths…* has won praise among historians but has gotten little notice outside of academe.

2. Among the sects were Anglicans, Calvinists, Congregationalists, Baptists, Dutch Reformed, Quakers, Lutherans, Presbyterians, Roman Catholics, Mennonites, Methodists, Moravians, Anabaptists, the Brethren, Sandemanians, Antinomians, Arminians, Shakers, Universalists, Antisabbatarians, Socinians, and Ranters.

3. For example, Maryland imposed severe penalties by law on anyone who denied the divinity of Jesus, the trinity, or the virgin birth.

4. Traditional Christians included Patrick Henry, Samuel Adams, Elias Boudinot, and John Jay. Christian Deists included John Adams, George Washington, Benjamin Franklin, Thomas Jefferson, and James Monroe. Non-Christian Deists included Tom Paine and Ethan Allen.

5. David L. Holmes, *The Faiths...*, p. 17)

6. The founders were all deeply influenced by the writings of John Locke (1632-1704), including his *Letter Concerning Toleration, First Treatise of Government*, and *Second Treatise of Government*.

Unbelief and the Vote

Tom Shipka (2007)

A pressing issue for many people in the United States today is whether Americans will vote for a Caucasian woman or an African-American man for president. (1) The answer is "Yes." Ninety percent of adult Americans say that, in principle, they are willing to vote for such candidates. When it comes to another category - unbelievers - the results are drastically different. Fifty-four percent of Americans say that they "would be unlikely" to vote for an atheist or agnostic. The percentage rises even higher among those respondents who profess a religion.

These revelations, disappointing if not surprising, come from a study by three researchers at the University of Minnesota that reports the attitudes of religious people in the United States toward nonreligious people. Based on a telephone survey of more than two thousand households and in-depth interviews with a sample from this group, the study shows that most believers:

- won't consider a presidential candidate who is an atheist or agnostic,
- hold that religion is central to being a good American and a good person,
- do not trust unbelievers,
- view unbelievers as selfish and uncaring, and
- oppose their children marrying unbelievers.

Nevertheless, the Minnesota study, which was published in the April 2006 *American Sociological Review*, shows a modest improvement in toleration of unbelievers in recent decades.

Further, on March 31 of this year, *Newsweek* released a poll that shows a trend of softening attitudes by believers toward unbelievers, alongside a residual refusal to seriously consider religious skeptics as candidates for public office. The Princeton Survey Research Associates International, which conducted the poll for *Newsweek*, contacted 1,004 adults aged eighteen or older. The poll finds that 68 percent of the respondents believe that a person can be moral and an atheist to 26 percent who said it is not possible. Furthermore, it reports that 49 percent of Americans report personally knowing an atheist and 47 percent believe that the nation is more accepting of atheists than it used to be. Nevertheless, it also found that most Americans - 62 percent - wouldn't vote for an atheist.

Despite this modest progress, mainstream views in the United States about the importance of belief in God are, to put it mildly, worrisome. In the first place, they fly in the face of these facts:

- Article VI of the Constitution says that "no religious test shall ever be required as a qualification to any office or public trust under the United States."
- Our political system is built upon the separation of church and state.
- The word *God* does not appear in the Constitution even once.
- Many of our Founders, including Thomas Jefferson, repudiated traditional religion.
- Thirty million or more Americans profess no religion.

In the second place, these views denigrate atheists and agnostics, many of whom lead responsible, productive, and even exemplary lives.

On this point, let me identify some prominent non-believers. Bill Gates and Warren Buffet, two of the richest people in the world, are also arguably its two greatest living philanthropists. Ted Turner, founder of CNN, gave a billion dollars to the United Nations. Actor Angelina Jolie, a United Nations Goodwill Ambassador, has invested her time and wealth in refugees and children in Africa and Asia. Many other respected actors, past and present, are also unbelievers. They include Diane Keaton, Keanu Reeves, Jodie Foster, Jack Nicholson, Margot Kidder, John Malkovich, Christopher Reeve, George C. Scott, Charles Laughton, and Katherine Hepburn. Musical artists Barry Manilow, Billy Joel, Frank Zappa, and James Taylor are unbelievers, as are Las Vegas headliners Penn and Teller, comedians Julia Sweeney and George Carlin, humor columnist Dave Barry, and *60 Minutes* curmudgeon Andy Rooney.

Further, non-believers also include American inventor Thomas Edison; Nobel laureates Francis Crick and James Watson, co-discoverers of DNA; economist Milton Friedman; chemist Linus Pauling; poet Robert Frost; playwright George Bernard Shaw; Gene Roddenberry, creator of *Star Trek*; Ernest Hemingway, one of America's greatest writers; A. Philip Randolph, African-American civil rights leader and founder of the Brotherhood of Sleeping Car Porters, the first black labor union in the United States; cyclist extraordinaire Lance Armstrong; long-distance swimmer Diana Nyad; golfer Annika Sorenstam; former Ohio State and Minnesota Vikings running back Robert Smith; and Hall-of-Fame baseball player

Ted Williams, who gave up nearly five full years of baseball during his prime to serve his country as a flight instructor and a fighter pilot in two wars. (So much for the no-atheists-in-foxholes canard.) Hundreds of more names could be added to these. (2)

Finally, while the Minnesota study and the *Newsweek* poll show that believers are quick to caricature or even demonize non-believers, one wonders if they also show that believers are impervious to the dark side of religion. Believers continue to feel confident that religion furnishes an accurate and reliable moral compass, despite religion's role in anti-Semitism, the Crusades, the Inquisition, religious wars, witch hunts, slavery, clergy sex abuse, the terrorist acts of September 11, 2001, and others, the subordination of women, the genital mutilation of girls, honor killings, violence against workers at women's clinics, fakery by faith-healers, the exploitation of believers by money-grubbing televangelists who, as the country-music lyric says, "tell you to send your money to God but give you their address," exacerbating conflict around the world, including sectarian violence, and the flimsy moral agenda of the religious Right, limited as it is to subversion of the principle of the separation of church and state and opposition to homosexuality, gay marriage, abortion, the teaching of evolution, and stem-cell research.

In a letter on the occasion of the fiftieth anniversary of American independence, Thomas Jefferson wrote: "May it (American's new form of government) be to the world, what I believe it will be: the signal of arousing men to burst the chains under which monkish ignorance and superstition had persuaded them to bind themselves, and to assume the blessings and security of self-government."

On that day, when America's intoxication with religion subsides and Americans judge candidates for public office on the basis of their character, intelligence, and commitment to public service, instead of whether they profess a preferred religious perspective, the Constitution will triumph, the nation will benefit, and Jefferson's hope will be realized. (3)

1. This article is reprinted with permission from *Free Inquiry*, October/November 2007, Vol. 27, No. 6, pp. 56-57. It was written and published in fall 2007 when Barack Obama and Hillary Clinton were battling for the Democratic nomination for President of the United States.

2. Don't get me wrong. I am *not* saying that all atheists and agnostics are pillars of virtue. For instance, shock-jock Howard Stern, *Hustler* magazine publisher Larry Flynt, and Karl Rove, President George W. Bush's alter ego, are not on my Super Bowl party invitation list. (That's right, friends, Karl Rove is an agnostic.) I *am* saying that whether a person does or does not profess

religion tells us nothing about his or her character or whether he or she enhances the lives of others. It's high time for people on both sides of the religious divide to recognize this.

3.   For additional information about politics and non-believers, see Brian Braiker, "God's Numbers," *Newsweek*, March 31, 2007; Penny Edgell, Joseph Gerteis, and Douglas Hartmann. "Atheists as Other: Moral Boundaries and Cultural Membership in American Society," *American Sociological Review* 71, Number 2, April 2006; and Francis FitzGerald, "The Evangelical Surprise." *The New York Review of Books*, April 26, 2007.

ABOUT THE AUTHOR:

Tom Shipka received his Ph.D. in philosophy from Boston College in 1969. That same year he began a 46-year career on the faculty at Youngstown State University. Early in his YSU career he spearheaded the unionization of the faculty and served as a leader of the faculty union for many years. Later, he served as Chair of the Department of Philosophy and Religious Studies. At YSU he was also a member and chair of the Academic Senate and active in fund-raising for both academic and athletic divisions of the university. Off campus he served as chair of the higher education councils of the Ohio Education Association and the National Education Association as well as chair of the NEA Higher Education Caucus and the Ohio Faculty Council. He is a three-time recipient of the YSU Distinguished Professor Award for achievements in teaching and scholarship and a two-time recipient of the YSU Watson Award for administrative service. He is an inductee of the YSU Heritage Society and the YSU Athletics Hall of Fame as a contributor, and a speakers series at the university is named in honor of him and his deceased father, a labor leader and YSU trustee.

He has also served on the boards of community organizations, including the Western Reserve Transit Authority, the Public Library of Youngstown and Mahoning County, and the Mill Creek MetroParks.

His publications include *Philosophy: Paradox and Discovery*, Fifth Edition, 2004; *Beliefs and Practices: Taking a Fresh Look*, Original Edition, 2016; *Commentaries: 162 Essays on WYSU*, 2018; and dozens of articles in social and political thought, critical thinking, and higher education labor relations.

Made in the USA
Columbia, SC
10 March 2018